WOMEN OF BRITAIN

WOMEN *of* BRITAIN

Letters from England

WITH RUNNING COMMENTARY BY
BEATRICE CURTIS BROWN

AND AN INTRODUCTION BY
JAN STRUTHER

NEW YORK
HARCOURT, BRACE AND COMPANY

ACKNOWLEDGMENT

I want to thank all those who have so kindly sent us their friends' letters for inclusion in this book, and have helped us in the deletion of certain personal details in order to preserve the writers' anonymity. It has not been possible in all cases to ask the writers themselves for permission to print the letters, but, judging by the way in which their friends over here have described them to us, and also by the tone of the letters themselves, I should guess that they are people who would do anything they possibly could to help to give the inhabitants of other countries a true picture of wartime life in Great Britain; and I can imagine no better means of doing this than by allowing the circulation of these personal letters. I hope, therefore, that I shall be forgiven for taking their permissions for granted; and that they will allow me to offer them my warmest thanks on behalf of the air-raid victims to whose relief the royalties of this book are to be devoted.

JAN STRUTHER

CONTENTS

CONTENTS

INTRODUCTION
by
JAN STRUTHER

INTRODUCTION

Here in New York it has been a lovely day—the kind of spring-in-winter day which in London always made me look out of the window to see if the lime-tree in the back garden was showing any sign of life. From force of habit I did the same thing here, only of course it was a sumach I was looking at instead of a lime-tree. I don't know the habits of sumachs, or when the first leaf-buds are likely to appear. That is the kind of thing which makes a country seem strange, however much one feels at ease with the human inhabitants of it. I am getting to know and to love this country; but one cannot completely love either countries or people until one has shared with them all moods, weathers, and seasons. *In sickness and in health, in summer and in autumn, in winter and in spring* . . .

When I first sat down to work this morning the sun was behind the "El" and all the southbound trains were packed with people going downtown to work. The Second Avenue families had got their washing hung out, and there was one particularly charming line-full with three little blue striped frocks and three little scarlet plaid frocks, going down in steps like the three bears. I guessed that they must belong to the Italian newsagent's

[3]

children round the corner. Anyway, they looked very gay and fluttery, and the spike on the top of the Chrysler Building was shining like a sword, and the man who lives on the top floor of the house opposite this one, beyond the sumach, was up on the roof as usual exercising his pigeons, waving a long flexible bamboo cane and making them fly round and round in circles, like a ringmaster.

But now the sun has just gone down beyond the Empire State, and it is the uptown trains that are full. I can see the rows of people in them, sitting or strap-hanging. They are going back to their own homes—in Queens, in Long Island City—and when they get there they will sleep all night in their own beds until it is time to get up and go to work again. The Chrysler Building, standing up black against a watermelon-pink sky, has ceased to be a petrified spring onion and become an elegant and elongated minaret. The pigeons have gone to roost in their wood-and-wire-netting pent-house, and their owner has just switched on the light in the room opposite to this one and is sitting peacefully eating his supper, with the evening paper propped up against a milk-bottle. It is a pleasant, ordinary, domestic scene. If it weren't for the skyscrapers in the background I might easily be looking in at one of the windows of that little row of houses behind ours in London, where the old chimney-sweep used to live: only he'd have been eating fish and chips instead of bolony, and instead of a milk-bottle there would have been a brown earthenware tea-pot. I've seen him sitting like that so many times, when I've got up to draw the curtains after tea, and I certainly never thought that that scene was going to become, in retrospect, the symbol of a whole chapter out of our lives. It was just one of the things one took for granted.

And oh! what a lot of those things there were. When I and my contemporaries first grew up, just about the time of the 1918 Armistice, some of us even took for granted that there would never be another war. That illusion didn't last long: but for many years after we had got accustomed to the idea that another war might come, we went on taking for granted that if it did come it would follow the familiar pattern of the war which had formed the background of our school-days. There would be bands playing, and flags flying, and lumps in the throat as one watched the columns of troops marching along Buckingham Palace Road in the direction of Waterloo or Victoria Station, singing the current "Tipperary," with their buttons shining as brightly as their eyes. There would be a well-established Expeditionary Force in Flanders. There would be a front line, and a second line, and billets in farm-houses, and Brigade Headquarters in old châteaux, and forty-eight hours' leave in Paris. There would be definite battles, with a beginning, a middle and an end; and after the battles there would be long casualty lists in *The Times*. At home, there would be military hospitals, and V.A.D.s, and recruiting stations, and charity concerts, and knitting parties, and bandage-rolling parties, and the brave old lady sitting under the cedar-tree on a summer afternoon watching the parlour-maid coming across the lawn with a telegram in her hand. There would be a spate of war marriages, some happy, some disastrous, and a flood of war poetry, much magnificent, much mediocre. As for the actual horrors— the blood, the screaming, the smashed skull, the spilled brain, the torn-off limb, the splintered bone jagging through flesh and skin—we should guess at these through the cuts in the news-reels or catch a glimpse of them in the eyes of men on leave: but they would not come nearer to us than that. Our job would be—as it was in the last war—to Keep the Home Fires Burning.

These were some of the things we took for granted. We knew that if war came it was bound to be a tragic and terrible business, but we did not envisage—how could we?—a war such as this one has become: a war in which brass buttons are as rare as brass bands, in which there are few songs and little poetry, in which the top floor attic is the front line, in which you are almost as likely to meet a war widower as a war widow, and in which the civilian's part is not so much to keep the home fires burning as to put out the incendiary bombs which threaten to burn down the homes themselves.

Above all, we did not envisage a war in which the entire domestic life of one of the most domesticated countries in the world would be turned inside out and upside down. In spite of the recent heavy bombardments, there are still comparatively few homes which have been physically destroyed by fire or high explosives: but there is scarcely a habitation in the land—scarcely a cottage or a castle, a luxury flat or a tenement dwelling, a country vicarage or a suburban villa, a back-to-back or a but-and-ben—which has not been forced to change the whole rhythm and pattern of its daily life. In the "safe" country districts, childless households have suddenly had to be reorganized to receive evacuated children, accompanied sometimes by a homesick and bewildered mother. Houses which already contained a few children have been stretched somehow in order to squeeze in several more. In the cities, young married couples whose lives had consciously or unconsciously revolved around the high wire safety-guard in front of the nursery hearth, and who had often wished that their house was a little larger and a little more sound-proof, have suddenly found themselves living in the midst of unwonted space, uncanny silence: and have wondered, perversely, how they ever came to grumble about the inconvenience of the perambulator in the narrow front hall. Very often, either for company's sake or in order to save expense, two of these young couples have decided to share a house together: and that, of course, has raised some pretty problems of adjustment. Moreover, at the beginning of this war, and even before it, innumerable men of what used to be called "the officer class" threw up their jobs and joined up eagerly in the ranks: so that many a woman who had been comfortably off and had been used to running a household has found herself having to live on the separation allowance of a private soldier's wife; which has meant, in many cases, shutting up her house and going to live as a "refugee" with relatives or friends. And all this, mind you, does not take into account the real refugees of the Blitzkrieg—the people whose dwellings have been demolished or made uninhabitable by bombing and who have lost all or part of their material possessions.

No, this certainly wasn't our idea of war. In war, our upbringing had led us to suppose, the men would go away to fight in order to defend their homes; while they were fighting (always, of course, on foreign soil) they would sustain themselves with the thought of their wives and children gathered every evening as usual around their own fireside, waiting for them to return; and when they did return—missing an arm or a leg, perhaps, but always victorious—they would walk up familiar steps, turn the handle of a familiar door and catch the first sight of their dear ones against a familiar background, with everything just as it used to be, nobody missing and no strangers present. *For England, Home and Duty. There's No Place Like Home. An Englishman's Home Is His Castle.* The old sweet catch phrases died hard. We certainly never imagined a war in which the homes themselves would be changed almost beyond recognition.

Yet that is the kind of war which it has turned out to be: and that is the kind of war of which these letters give so moving a picture. And when I use the word "moving" I mean it in both senses: for the picture is not only profoundly touching, it is also startlingly alive.

This disruption of family life is probably the greatest ordeal which the people of Great Britain could have been called upon to undergo. As a nation we tend to stay put, to go on living in the same house for years and years—generally, in fact, until births or deaths have made the family either too large or too small for it. Leases can be drawn up for pretty well as long as one likes, and they run from whatever date one chooses to sign them. We have no special "Moving Day," such as there is here in New York, when half the population seems to join in a light-hearted game of General Post and when loaded furniture vans blunder all over the city like bumble bees. That is a phenomenon at which most English people would be both surprised and puzzled. In England, when at last it becomes necessary to change houses, it is the fashion to throw up one's hands and groan. We have a saying, "Three moves is as bad as a fire." And I remember that once, when a London cook of ours got a description of the First of October in a letter from her sister in Manhattan, she just shook her head in bewilderment and said: "It don't seem natural to me, summow. I mean, your 'ome's your 'ome."

Your home's your home. Yes, but what *is* your home? In England we do not use the word, as people do over here, to mean simply a house. We never talk about buying a home: we talk about buying (or renting) a house and *making* a home. There are three dimensions to a house, but four to a home; and the fourth is time.

That is why this war has struck more intimately into

[9]

the heart of England than any other war—even those
fought on her own soil. And that is why we can be quite
certain that her people will see it through to the end.
For when people are fighting only because they love
their dwelling-places, there is always the danger that a
moment may come when they will surrender in order
to protect those very dwelling-places from destruction.
But when a nation has already had the greater part of
its home life disrupted, transplanted or indefinitely suspended, and it still goes on fighting and enduring, then
we know that it is fighting for something more precious
than bricks and mortar, more precious even than its own
home life—that is, it is fighting for the *idea* of home life,
for the right of all human beings to live how and where
they like, and to sit round the fire in the evenings reading what they like, listening to what they like, or saying
what they like, without pricking an ear for the tramp
of boots or the peremptory knock on the door. When
this right has been re-established, and not before, the
people of Great Britain will pick up the tune of their
own home life where it was interrupted. They can afford to wait—the rhythm of it runs so strongly in their
heads.

II

Woman's place, nowadays, is by no means only in the
home: but it is inevitable, even now, that any change
or disturbance in the home life of a nation should affect the women even more deeply than the men. For
this reason, we have confined ourselves in this book to

letters from women. And that is why, also, we have not picked out isolated pages or paragraphs which describe some incident directly connected with the war, but have printed the whole letter whenever we possibly could. This, we felt, was the only way of giving the reader a fair and well-balanced picture of what life in Great Britain is like at the present time—the only way to get the ordinariness and the extraordinariness of it all in true proportion. We have included, also, some letters which have hardly anything to do with the war at all: because it is so deeply significant that people who are living in such conditions *can* write letters which have hardly anything to do with the war. The point is that these "peaceful" letters—as anybody who reads them will admit —are not written in a spirit of escapism: their detachment springs from the inner sanity and serenity of the people who wrote them—from their deep-rooted, though often unconscious, conviction that the normal commonplace things they write about are the things that really matter in the end.

These letters are, of course, all *real* letters; and nothing has been altered—except to render them as anonymous as possible. Brief indications have been given of the age, occupation and general background of the writers, because this obviously adds to the interest; but names of people have usually been reduced to an initial and a full stop, names of places to an initial and a dash. The names of children have usually been left in full, to differentiate them from grown-ups; otherwise many of the

comments and anecdotes would seem pointless. Occasional variations from these rules will be readily explained
by the context. The places of origin have had to be
treated with a certain discretion. The names of large
cities have been printed in full, but in the case of small
towns and villages only the county has been given.

In two or three cases we have had the good fortune to
be given access to a whole series of letters from the same
person in England to the same correspondent in America, and we have of course kept these letters together.
Some of them give a connected story of external events,
others throw an interesting light on the changes in spirit
and mental outlook which took place during succeeding
phases of the war. Except for these series, the letters in
each section of the book are in chronological order, but
the book as a whole is not arranged chronologically. We
thought it more interesting to divide the writers in various ways, sometimes according to age, sometimes according to habitat, sometimes according to social background
—in order to illustrate the impact of the war upon different groups of people in a highly intricate modern
civilization.

Those who read this book straight through will soon
find themselves recognizing certain themes which recur
again and again. The main one, as I have said, is the
temporary disruption of family life, the separation of
husbands from wives and parents from children; the sudden disappearance of a familiar background. The writers
react to this in various ways, some with bewilderment,

some with resignation, some with relief at finding how little difference this separation makes to their feeling of unity as a family. "It makes me so *angry*," says one on page 124, "that the world should be in this state where one can't be with one's husband or child in one's own home." A luckier one, on page 134, writes: "We are so amazingly blessed in being able to be all together in our own home, not scattered like so many families—and what does an evacuee or so matter in comparison with that?" A third, who has gone to live with a houseful of relatives and who has just had a baby, says cheerfully, "The one merciful thing is that now I have Lucia I am much less cross and have quite forgotten that I ever had a home of my own or any snug place like that, so that life is far more liveable." But it is a sentence on page 69 which hits the nail squarest on the head. "I used to be afraid," says this writer (who had been married only a year when war broke out and to whom housekeeping was still a romantic adventure)—"I used to be afraid that when we hadn't a home it would upset and unsettle us—the house meant so much in our life together. But I can see now it isn't going to. We've got something far more permanent and solid even than a house—though I wouldn't like not to have one *just as soon as we can* again, when peace comes."

Another important theme is the effect of the war upon children—which was not always, by any means, what their parents had expected it to be. Students of child psychology will have their work cut out to draw any definite conclusions from the conflicting scraps of evidence which they will find in this book. The story of Sue's first air raid, for instance, on page 94; the little boy and his sister on page 139; and the children watching air battles from their rock caves on page 151. As for the letter from the ten-year-old girl on page 324, it deserves to become immortal, if only for the terrible and touching simplicity of its conclusion:

"Send Pog my love. The fireworks are still going on outside and now I have to go to my little bed under the dresser. If it wasn't for old Nasty I should be in a comfortable bed."

Food of course is a constantly recurring topic. Not because of any general shortage, but because to ration meat, in a country whose chief culinary pride and interest is in the cooking of meat, is to change the dietetic habits of the whole country. I think most people would agree that the change has been for the better. Certainly the fact that it became impossible, even for those who could afford it, to buy whole joints of beef and mutton, meant that English housewives were forced to concentrate their skill and ingenuity upon the preparation of other foods which they had always tended to neglect. A wise, charming and Anglophile French woman, who escaped across the Channel by the skin of her teeth and who is now doing Red Cross work in London, was heard to remark: "By the time the war is over, this country will be *quite* perfect. It will not only have defeated Hitler, it will also have learnt how to cook vegetables."

There are two letters in this book from an English children's nurse, and throughout the other letters there will be found occasional references to Nannies. This gives me an opportunity to put right a misconception which exists over here about our "nursery nurses." I find that to most Americans the word "Nannie" conjures up a picture of a terrifying old dragon with a grey tweed suit and a black felt hat, who tyrannizes over her employers, offends the cook, and either spoils or intimidates the children under her care. This formidable type may have been common fifty or sixty years ago. Even thirty years ago, in my own childhood, I seem to remember a certain number of my contemporaries having that kind of nurse. (I felt sorry for them—my own was a humorous, loving, free-and-easy woman, who used to let me buy hot baked potatoes from the street-seller at the corner and take them to bed with me on cold foggy London nights.) Even today a few of the tweed dragons still exist: I have seen them occasionally at the grander and more elaborate kind of children's party. But on the whole, nowadays, English Nannies are pleasant, adaptable, good-humoured people, who dress well, talk intelligently, are on good terms with both the cook and the employer, and treat the children with affectionate understanding and common sense. Sometimes one is lucky enough to find a Nannie who is all this and a great deal more; who—while keeping her own individuality and opinions—identifies herself with the fortunes of the family, shares all its ups and downs, and in the course of years becomes an invaluable friend and adviser. If one has ever had that sort of luck, one naturally wants to make sure that people in other countries don't have the wrong ideas about English Nannies.

The English have never made themselves out to be a particularly musical race: but throughout these letters the subject of music keeps on cropping up. I remember how many of us, during the anxious and bewildered time of the Munich crisis, turned, or returned, to music as a source of comfort and serenity; and since the war began this tendency has been even more noticeable. The wild success of the National Gallery concerts is enough to prove that. But people do not only go to concerts, or listen to broadcasts or recorded music. They have also recaptured their old, and nearly lost, delight in making their own music at home. As everybody knows who has even been part of one, it doesn't particularly matter whether a family orchestra or a family choir performs well or not. The point of the thing is in the doing of it: and it is one of the most fascinating occupations in the world. I know one household at least whose distress at being separated was intensified by the fact that this meant breaking up the family string quartet. On the other hand, there were many houses where the presence of extra guests or evacuees made it all the easier to get up some kind of music-making in the evenings.

Just before I came over here I went to stay with some relatives in Edinburgh. Two other friends came in after supper, and the five of us spent several hours singing—

or trying to sing—old English madrigals. It was a beautiful warm light midsummer evening; the windows were wide open and the scent of red hawthorn came floating in from the gardens on the other side of the granite-setted street. We sat round, happy and absorbed, completely at one, weaving anew in the air patterns of sound which were three or four hundred years old. I remember thinking, suddenly, "*This* is what we are fighting for." And when we finally stopped, my brother-in-law said, "I've just realized—I haven't thought about the news for three hours." Nor had any of us. It was just about the time of the fall of France.

Another thing worth noticing is the frequent remarks about "foreign refugees"—i.e. the racial or political exiles who had come over to England to escape from persecution in Nazi territory. These remarks were always friendly, often affectionate, even when the Government internment scheme was in full swing and certain hysterical newspapers were trying to foster an indiscriminate witch-hunt for Fifth Columnists. Anybody who was in England at that time, and who made a study of the subject, knows that the general attitude of the so-called "enemy aliens" towards internment was marvellously reasonable, patient and long-sighted. Over and over again I have heard them express, in various ways, this opinion: "Nobody has better reason than we have for detesting Hitler and all that he stands for. We love your country and we long to help you to defeat Nazism. We would rather, of course, be allowed to take up arms and fight for

you, but if the only way we can help is by all being interned in order that your government may catch the few
Nazi agents who managed to slip in with us disguised
as refugees, then let us be interned with a good grace,
and get the whole thing over as soon as possible." It
was one of the peculiar ironies of this war that such a
measure had to be introduced, and the carrying out of
it involved many unnecessary separations and hardships,
but on the whole it is reassuring to see how comparatively little bitterness it caused on either side. Read, for
instance, on page 261, about "poor A.," whose employer
would "miss her dreadfully if she has to go" but thinks
it is right all the same. And read, on page 183, about
Aunt L. (an elderly lady) who "persists in staying on
at her flat in London, although they've had an awful
lot of damage round there, chiefly because the refugee
cook can't leave her restricted area and she doesn't want
to leave her alone." It's certainly a queer war.

Naturally, there are many references to the U. S. A.,
especially in those letters which were written round
about the time when the British Government was trying to work out a practicable scheme for the transat-
lantic evacuation of children. This scheme had to be
abandoned for lack of convoy ships, but during the
weeks when it was under discussion a good deal of so-
called "private evacuation" took place. That is to say,
there were thousands of parents in Great Britain who
could afford (some easily, some with great difficulty) to
send their children over to the United States without

Government assistance, and whose friends and relatives
over on this side had been begging them for months to
do so. It is interesting to study the answers to these
invitations. Gratitude was uppermost, of course—gratitude all the more heartfelt because the people of England knew from experience what it meant to undertake
the work and responsibility of looking after evacuated
children. Yet over and over again these offers were
regretfully declined. Various reasons were given: that
the parents couldn't bear to part with them; that the
crossing was too risky; that "Europeans ought to stay in
Europe"; that "we don't want the next generation to
grow up to feel they can escape anything unpleasant by
going away." But these were not the only considerations
that held parents back. To my certain knowledge, there
were many who, much as they longed to send their own
children to safety, felt that it would not be fair to do so
while there were millions of parents in the country for
whom such a thing was a financial impossibility. When
the Government evacuation scheme was announced,
these parents heaved a sigh of relief and considered themselves at last free to go ahead with the plans which they
had been longing to carry out. Indeed, it seemed to them
that the sooner they sent their children over here the
better, so that they would not be competing for space
on the boats when the Government scheme finally got
under way. As I have said, the scheme fell through:
clearly no government could take the responsibility of
backing such a scheme unless adequate convoys could be

provided: and that, it seems, was impossible. But before it was finally abandoned hundreds of mothers had brought their children over here at their own expense and at their own risk, and thousands more had sent them unaccompanied, believing in all good faith that the "public" evacuees were to follow shortly, and that there would not be a family in Great Britain, whatever its income or its social status, whose children would not have an equal chance of crossing the Atlantic. When the complicated psychological history of this war comes to be written, that is one of the misunderstandings which will need to be cleared up.

The abortive Government evacuation scheme had at least one invaluable effect: it proved beyond all possible doubt how deep, genuine and warm-hearted is the sympathy which the American people feel towards the people of Great Britain. For in what seemed like the twinkling of an eye homes were thrown open in the U. S. A. to no less than five million potential refugee children. Offers poured in from all over the country—not only from the Atlantic Seaboard, where the ties with England are commonly supposed to be the strongest, but from the far South, the Middle West, the Pacific Coast. It was an amazing and generous gesture of welcome: a gesture which will never be forgotten, even though it proved impossible to accept more than a small fraction of the offers of hospitality.

On page 269, in the group called "Decisions and Changes," there is one letter which will be of outstand-

ing interest to both American and English readers. For
it not only states more explicitly than the rest the reasons
why some parents felt that they should not send their
children abroad at the present time: it also conveys, more
clearly than I have yet seen it conveyed anywhere else,
the spirit with which Great Britain is accepting the material changes that the war has brought about. The writer
points out how difficult it would be to live lavishly over
here for the duration of the war and then go back to the
comparative poverty which she sees will be inevitable
in Great Britain for a long time to come. There is so
much to be learnt in England just now, she says: and
she feels that the children ought to stay and learn it too,
so that they may be better equipped to inhabit the world
of the future. These are serious and moving words, which
might well be taken to heart by many, and not least by
those of us who, after deep soul-searchings, made the
opposite decision and brought our children away from
the zone of war. Reading this letter, we can see clearly
once and for all the goal towards which many of us have
been groping ever since we landed. We have got to find
some way of bringing up our children over here in safety
and comfort without unfitting them to take their place
as citizens of a post-war England. We have got to keep
them in constant touch with the changes of outlook
which are taking place at home; help them to readjust
their values; and above all, teach them not to take for
granted the material ease of life in this country (which
might here, as elsewhere, vanish overnight) but to look

below the surface and discover the enduring framework upon which these draperies are hung. This framework is made up of the sturdy and independent spirit of the men and women who built America—the early settlers, the makers of the Revolution, the explorers, the prospectors, the pioneers. I would have all British children over here encouraged to learn as much as possible—by story-books, by good moving pictures, and by word of mouth—about American history, because I believe there is no better way of preparing them for the task of rebuilding Europe, in which, eventually, they will be privileged to take a hand; the task of re-civilizing a deliberately de-civilized continent, in which reason and justice have been replaced by the ethics of the poisoned arrow and the scalping-knife. It will be a pioneer's job: it is going to need a high degree of courage, endurance, self-denial, strength of spirit and singleness of mind. These are austere qualities. It is hard enough to learn them, or to teach them, even in the midst of rationing and bombardment: it is harder still in the midst of plenty and security. But if we fail—if we allow ourselves and our children to regard our life over here as a temporary escape from unpleasantness, rather than as a preparation for strenuous adventure—then we shall have forfeited our right to enjoy the blessings of safety.

Probably one of the most remarkable things about these letters is the fact that they were written at all. As everybody knows, the art of letter-writing has been in decay for a long time. People are busier nowadays than they used to be. Externally, there are so many more things which it is possible to do. But while the choice of pastimes and occupations has grown wider and wider, the length of a day has remained obstinately 24 hours: so that the amount of time which people have felt inclined to devote to letter-writing has steadily dwindled. Besides, other methods of communication have improved so rapidly during the past twenty years. Travel has become quicker and cheaper. If you want to exchange ideas with your friends, it has been comparatively easy to go and visit them: easier still to telephone. But the war has changed all this. Travel is slow, expensive and sometimes impossible. Telephone systems are over-burdened and often disorganized. Even before night raids had put an end to outdoor expeditions after dark, the black-out had been encouraging the general public to spend their evenings at home; while the members of the various Air Raid Precautions services had to fill in many, many hours at their stations, on duty yet inactive, always awaiting the signal for a practice alarm— which at any time might turn out to be a real one. (And here is another chapter which will have to be written in that psychological history—written by somebody who knows how to pay a proper tribute to the sticking power of those A.R.P. workers between September 1939 and June 1940. It is one thing—and a very great thing—to stick to your job in times of terror and danger: it is another— and possibly a greater—to stick to it in times of boredom and bathos. For bathos was the keynote of those months

especially for the A.R.P. workers. They had joined up at
the outbreak of war, or earlier, burning with enthusiasm,
eager to learn any job, however difficult and dangerous,
and expecting—as we all did—immediate air attack of
the most violent kind. Instead, nothing happened. Nothing happened. Their uniforms—which had not been
smart or glamorous even when new—grew shabby. Their
brown or dark blue denim boiler-suits faded a little and
shrank in the wash. Worst of all, their jobs ceased to be
news. Their families' eyes glazed over when they talked
shop. There were letters to the papers from optimistic
busybodies criticizing the A.R.P. services as a piece of
wanton and scarey extravagance on the part of an alarm-
ist Government. The average A.R.P. worker at that period
felt bored, misunderstood, short of sleep, cut off from
much social intercourse by changing hours of shifts, and
more than a little irritated by the faces, voices and man-
nerisms of the small group of equally bored, sleepy and
irritable people with whom he or she had to spend 8 or
12 hours out of the 24 in ill-lit draughty garages or in
small smoke-filled rooms. Yet they stuck it, practically
all of them: and in the light of what has happened since,
the rest of us can see what a debt we owe them.)

All this, and the fact that so many families were for-
cibly split up, led to a miraculous revival of the custom
of letter-writing. I should dearly love to know some statis-
tics about the number and length of the private letters
which were written in Great Britain during the first nine
months of this war. And the habit, once begun, was

kept up even after the Blitzkrieg began. All this, perhaps, is fairly natural: but what is remarkable is the
style in which most of the letters are written. The British are supposed to be, in general, an inarticulate race,
shy of expressing emotion, shyer still of putting their be-
liefs and theories into words. Yet read through these letters, and you will find not only scattered sentences which
move the heart "more than with a trumpet," but whole
paragraphs of the acutest perception, the frankest self-
analysis. And when you have read them all you will find
that from these sentences, these paragraphs, has emerged
the whole philosophy of a nation. It is not a portrait,
painted by one artist, but a mosaic picture, made up by
many hands out of small chippings from dozens of different lives. That is what makes it so poignant and so
revealing.

There is a strong temptation to quote. "I can assure
you," says one writer on page 91, "that many many ordinary people feel like I do and are neither too cynical nor
too self-conscious to feel proud of England. And it's quite
amazing—I never could have imagined it—how happy it
makes me and how I can enjoy every minute of each
day more intensely than ever before. Like being in love,
but more restful."

And here on page 112 is another notable comment:
"How gloriously adaptable we shall all be after the war!
S. and I used to make an awful fuss at a hotel if we could
only get a double-bedded room—and now we share a sin-

gle mattress on the floor in the greatest luxury. It must be good for one, obliquely."

Then there is an admirable bit of understatement on page 315, in a letter from the 70-year-old widow of a general:

"Last night I slept a whole night in my bed, *which was a most delightful experience.*" (The italics are mine.)

And a cheerful piece of fatalism on page 320: "At about 10 P.M. we go down to bed. And that is really more peaceful, because there is nothing more one can do, so it is no good worrying."

And there is this passage on page 319, which in its closing sentence sums up one lesson that the war has taught us: "Won't it be fun after the war; you must come over to help us celebrate even if we are by then living in tents! It is odd about a war, the things that don't really matter, don't matter one bit!"

But it is better, after all, to stop quoting, and to leave the reader to make his own discoveries and to draw his own conclusions. An American philosopher, after going right through the manuscript of this book in complete silence, laid it down and made one brief comment. "These people," he said, "are not only making history: they are writing history."

III

It is quite dark now. The "El" trains, both uptown and downtown, are practically empty. The newsagent's wife has long ago taken in the six little dresses from her line (I could hear the squeak of the pulley). The pigeon man has gone to bed. The lights in the skyscraper windows have been put out one by one like candles on a Christmas tree at the end of a party. Very soon it will be time to listen to the midnight news.

There are moments when one can almost feel the earth turning. Westward, in the big central farmlands, the night is an hour younger. Further west, in the cattle country, in the high plains and mountains, it is an hour younger still. On the Pacific coast, they have the whole evening before them. But three thousand miles to the eastward tomorrow's sun is already rising, and the people of England—the chimney-sweep, and the pigeon-fancier, and the newsagent, and their wives and children—are just waking up to face another day.

I

DAY TO DAY LIFE

DAY TO DAY LIFE

For a year before the war the women of England had
been carrying out their daily work with an eye on the
newspapers and an ear on the wireless. When an invitation came for two weeks ahead, they accepted it, thinking, "If we are still going to parties then—if war hasn't
come by then." Most of them had spent two or three
days a week at first aid classes, ambulance classes or
anti-gas classes. When they went to the grocer's for supplies, they were apt to get in an extra can of something,
for they were building up a small store of durable food
—just in case there should be a rush on the shops in an
emergency. Every now and then the pressure would
ease; they would eat up the extra stores recklessly. Out-
ings and days of pleasure were eagerly grasped at; every
familiar sight—the countryside, Kew Gardens in spring,
Piccadilly in the pale June light—was lingered over. From
"Munich time" on, month by month, the tension tight-
ened. In March came the taking of Prague: they wondered if Easter would be a holiday. But Easter passed
and the enchanting holiday of Whitsun, when buttercups spread over fields. Tentative holidays were taken in
June and July. Then August set in, first wet and cold
and then ominously heavy and hot. And towards the
end of August, they read in their morning paper "Russo-

German Pact signed" and knew that the end was very near.

Some people had bought their brown paper and drawing pins already; those who had not, went to the little stationer's shops around the corner and bought them. Brown paper, black paper, heavy dark curtains—anything in stock—for blacking out the windows and filling up the cracks in doors. Leaflets came through the door every hour, it seemed; kindly-worded unalarming leaflets, telling what to do when and if war should be declared; how to restrict your light, how to store food— not too much of it, just enough for three days' possible shortage. How to keep your gas masks safe. . . .

People talked about one thing; they were not very much frightened—not as they had been at the time of Munich. They talked quietly, with patience and with resignation. "Well, I suppose we've got to stop him, there won't be any peace till we do." Arrangements were made. "We're going to send Billy down to Cousin So-and-So's." "I'll stay here till George is called up and then I'm going into the Ambulance Service." "I think I know all the gases now—except that one which smells of mouse—I always forget that."

Then came the bad week when they waited by the radio all day and a good deal of the night. That week, notes went back and forth, from London to Berchtesgaden, from Warsaw to London, from Berchtesgaden to London. There was one worse fear than war . . . There was only one thing to speak of; at no time before or since the war has a nation's mind been concentrated on one thing so horribly, so uninterruptedly, as during that week.

And all through that week, the sun shone as it so rarely does in England in August. The wet spring and early summer had given the earth great freshness; there was no midsummer heaviness about the trees. All the summer flowers—lupins, delphiniums, stocks, roses and great heavy dahlias—were in full blossom. The earlier heaviness had lifted; now the sky was quite high and clear blue.

Every day they expected the final Note to pass, each day brought a kind of reprieve—till Friday morning, September 1st. That morning, instead of starting off the news with the weather report, the B.B.C. announcer opened with, "There is grave news this morning." Poland had been invaded.

That day and the next two days, there was almost no train travel for ordinary people, and cars were warned off the roads; the school children and the mothers with children under five were being evacuated from the large towns to the "safe" districts. Into the villages came trains loaded with bewildered, labelled children and with dazed mothers, dressed in their Sunday clothes, carrying the babies in their arms. They were herded into schools or town halls to wait, while the Women's Voluntary Services, and anyone else who was about, gave them cups of tea and tried to amuse the children. Then they were passed on to their "billets"—to the hosts who had undertaken to give homes to them. Some of the effects of this evacuation will be read in the letters following. Briefly it may be said that as far as the children were concerned, the evacuation scheme—one of the largest and most ambitious that have ever been put into practice—was a success. Certainly it was carried out with singularly few mishaps. So far as the mothers were concerned, however, it was not wholly satisfactory. Many of them worried about their husbands, left behind in the city to shift for themselves. They were ill at ease in their new homes, feeling that they were there only on sufferance—though as a rule the sufferance was kindly enough. Moreover, they were homesick for city life. In one village at least, they used to wheel their prams out to the main high road and wait for the hourly country bus to pass by—"just so as to see a bit of traffic." They did not, most of them, know how to accept gracefully; they were off their own ground and felt at a disadvantage. They resented the servants in the big houses where they were billeted, and the servants often made no bones about their own feelings toward the evacuees.

Most of these mothers had gone home by Christmas, in spite of earnest pleas put out on the radio and in the press by the Government. But the majority of the children stayed and grew taller and fatter and less pale in the face.

As for the middle-class wives—most of them, if they had children, evacuated themselves to week-end cottages or to relatives. Or they took small houses in the country. Some of them grew impatient or homesick and went back to town after a month or so. But few of them let their children go back. Each day might be the day that the Germans decided to send over their planes. Never for one day did that dread lift from people in England, for all the quietness that lay over the country during the first nine months of the war.

There were very few women whose entire life was not changed. Those who stayed in the city mostly worked at A.R.P. posts, ambulance driving, canteen work, W.V.S. and so on; if they were independent, they would undertake full-time duty; if they already had jobs, they would do part-time war-work after hours. Although there was apparently no immediate danger, women looked, by Christmas time, a little strained, very slightly drawn under the eyes. The double work, the black-out, the separation from husbands and families, were telling on them. But for all that, they were gay enough and they showed, perhaps, more lightness of heart than they had for the past year.

Those in the country were also working. As will be seen from the letters, they found plenty to do. Many plunged eagerly into vegetable gardening. Women who had lived all their lives in cities and knew nothing about the growing of vegetables, far less about cooking and canning them, became very proud housewives. They boasted about the rows of jampots on their shelves, they read agricultural papers and eagerly compared notes with every villager. Others were entirely absorbed in coping

with their evacuees. Others, again, took part in the local
A.R.P. work.

All sorts of strange modifications of life took place;
for instance, the car was no longer a familiar friend because petrol was rationed. People who had not bicycled
since their school-days took to doing so again. They cycled
six miles to tea and back, cycled into market and brought
their stores home in a basket slung over the handle bars.
They wore rubber boots because the winter was so hard
and because the price of shoes went up very soon after
the war. They lived in sweaters and tweeds.

The hardness of the winter was, that first year, almost
identified with the war itself. One child said, "We must
get rid of that old Hitler and then the snow will go."
There had not been such a winter in England, it was
said, for ninety years. Snow lay on the ground for two
months, even in the south. Coal deliveries were held up
because the railways were blocked with ice. Sometimes
food did not get through to the villages. Pipes froze and
burst. Neighbours, even in London, begged water from
each other.

Then the snow melted, the spring broke through and
ushered in the loveliest English summer that anyone
could remember. This too can be read of in the letters,
and the curious effect it had on people's feelings; the
sunshine and loveliness making a backcloth for the invasion of Holland, the invasion of France, the fall of
Paris.

LONDONERS IN EXILE

The first group in "Day to Day Life" is made up of letters from four young-middle-aged, upper-middle-class London women. They are the kind of women to be found in every metropolitan city: wives of professional, literary, official men; educated, thoughtful, gay, on the whole sophisticated. In London they would live mostly in houses rather than apartments; and would be almost as aware of New York or Paris as of London. Their political views would tend to be Liberal or further Left. They would be interested in pictures, music, books, movies, dance tunes, politics, flowers, their own houses and families, cooking, history, music-hall variety, social conditions.

This section, then, consists of a complete set of letters from four different people of the same group, writing among each other, which gives them a continuity and special interest. We begin with them because this kind of woman in England, as in every country, is articulate and reflective and expresses a general view—a view held by many who do not or cannot put it into words. Their letters are given in full here as much for the state of mind they describe, and for their reflections on events, as for the actual descriptions of the events themselves—which indeed are sometimes more dramatically and vividly described in letters found later in the book.

THE SOLDIER'S WIFE

The letters in this first group were written by a London woman, married only a year before. Her husband volunteered for the army on the outbreak of war; their income disappeared and she went as a "voluntary evacuee" to live with a friend in the country. This is an example which was fairly common, of a couple reduced, by the war, from a fairly comfortable income to a bare subsistence level of a private's pay—less than $6.50 a week ($5 allowance for the wife, $1.50 for the husband). As will be seen, they were compelled to give up their house and all their life together. The letters were written to the woman's mother in America, and cover the first eight months of the war, from the week before the outbreak to the invasion of Holland.

CHELSEA, LONDON
August 22, 1939

DARLING C.:

I am sitting on the front steps in hot sunshine beside a tub of fuchsias which kind E. contributed towards the garden, drying my hair. A. [the writer's husband] and I use the front steps the way Americans use a porch and just sit on it, because the sun comes down so hot there and we can see over the wire fence to Mrs. P.'s lovely garden (full of snapdragons, hollyhocks, petunias and violas and roses). The neighbours are so sweet and friendly here that they don't seem to think it brings down the tone of the street.

You know by the papers what a spot we are in. I needn't say it is entirely occupying our thoughts and sometimes this last few days it seemed more than one could bear. The Russian pact news today made me feel faint when I read it. But now we feel stronger again (inside I mean) and see that if we still do fight then it is because we have got rid of appeasement and licking Germany's boots, and it is because we have the guts to fight. So I suppose one must stick to that thought. A. is now out enquiring at a recruiting office. He won't enlist till war is declared but he wants to get into an artillery regiment so he is finding out beforehand. Yesterday we got black paper to darken our windows and got everything ready. I can't tell you how much better this is—at least for me and A.—than at Munich. We have had a year together, we have had a home. And now the time has come there has been time to make our plans, like darkening the house etc. and arranging to go to R.'s (for me). We know where we are. It's been a bad month, and every news from every side has been awful and crucial! I have felt knocked over dozens of times but I'm darned now if I can be got down. I feel so much more able to stand up than I did and though I'm scared to death of air raids, I believe when they come I'll be able to stand them.

SUSSEX
August 26, 1939

DARLING C.:

We are still waiting, so I am writing now in case I
am rather occupied for the next few days and can't get a
letter off. And I thought you would like to hear what
the past week has been like—for by the time you get this
something will have happened—peace or war—and there
will be no harm in your knowing! (I mean one hesitates
to discuss one's state of mind at the time because one
doesn't want to enhance anyone's depression, but after
a week's delay it doesn't matter!)

Last Monday we began to know that normal times
were over. I forget why now. Partly because August 21st
has been a date that was scheduled as the DATE for about
a month and because Halifax and Chamberlain had
said they were coming back to London then. Also there
may have been heavier troop movements in Germany.
I can't remember—it seems a month ago. The wireless
began giving "war" directions, about darkening houses,
etc., very calmly though. It was quite different from
September, no hysteria or crowds queueing up for gas
masks this time. P., on whom we so much rely, though
he can't tell us anything because he doesn't know, did
say, "It's going to be a bad week and it's even chances
for war," though he rather thought it wouldn't come.
Anyway it suddenly became immediately necessary to
do things. Tuesday we got our black paper and covered
our windows, bought a shovel and torch—I had already

[40]

got in a week's supply of tinned food. Blacking windows
was a good thing—occupied us and I felt, damn the war,
I've got to get this done first—it can wait till I'm finished.
Wednesday I turned out the house as usual (I have
been so thankful for housework). A. went to Hornsey
where the nearest artillery regiment is stationed and
found that he could probably get into it. He wanted to
be sure, because otherwise he'd be pushed into any regiment when he is called up and he wants specially to be
in artillery which is interesting at least and takes some
brains and skill—in fact where you can learn a trade
even if it is only handling a gun. He will be in the ranks
of course (this war isn't like the last one!).

Wednesday evening, when we did feel frightfully low,
T. called up and said it would be a good thing for us
to forgather and we were to dress and come round for
a drink and all go out. Wasn't it *lovely* of him! So we
did. It was a lovely hot night. (I must add that, making
everything doubly hard, the weather has been hot but
heavy and ominous and full of thunder "off.") So I put
on my wedding dress and we went and had martinis. I
proposed "to a good future" and dear T. looked very
sweet and grave and said "yes, that is our best toast."
Then we went to the Berkeley to eat (T.'s party, of
course) and then to the Gate Revue and then back to
his place where we played lovely gramophone records
of the best American band players and drank whisky.
Got home at 2:30 A.M. feeling fine.

Thursday my birthday. A. gave me a surprise. A white

[41]

vase with a pussy climbing out of it. But apart from
that, Thursday was the worst day. In the evening I
felt absolutely flattened out, hopeless and without any
resistance. The weather, as I said, was the kind that
gets you down—though it *looked* lovely. Also all the
time for the past 2 weeks the aeroplanes have increased.
All day long you hear them recrossing and recrossing
over your roof and it sort of got on one's nerves. Actually I forgot to say that one's state of mind fell bang
down on Tuesday with the Russian news. It made the
whole war seem futile and broke one's faith in everything. It was just a bloody old war that was going to
be difficult and no one except Chamberlain to lead us.
And we don't like him any better than we did.

But Thursday A. and I talked it over and said in spite
of *everything* we'd rather have a war than live like the
Germans do. It was less frightening to have an air raid
than to fear that an S.S. man would call at your door
and take you to concentration camp and to have your
friends disappear mysteriously and never to be able to
say what you thought or read or trust anyone. It is
BETTER. In my worst moments I have never felt otherwise. And we said, if Russia has left us, then if we go
to war it is because as a people we all believe in this,
and that is something worth going to war for; it means
we are better and healthier than we were last September. It is a voluntary act.

And we also said that we had had a good year and
nothing could upset us or disturb us or change the kind

of people that we were, which is a great comfort for us. It's queer how much people are saying that to each other—one thinks it is only oneself. But I found P. had written it to R. (he is in Paris now and she doesn't know quite when he will be back, poor lamb) and N. says it every time we telephone.

Friday, R. was coming up to town from L—— A—— and we were going back with her on our way to Bognor where we had planned a visit before the crisis ever happened. C. had rung up the night before—her theatrical Company had had no instructions and were planning to carry on until they were told to go. She didn't want to leave them but asked what I thought she should do. I said, don't come to London. (You see, London is going to be rather a mess because of the mass evacuation of poor people, all the trains and roads are going to be taken over by the Govt. to evacuate people and it is doubtful whether one will be able, for the first four days, to get in or out. Besides, food may be a problem.) So I told her to stay at Sheerness if she wanted to and if the company was broken up to go to the D.'s which she says she could easily reach as it is a cross country journey. Also we were worried about Father because if war breaks (as everyone thinks it will) tomorrow, Sunday, he may not be able to get to London. But A. said we could pick him up at Southampton and bring him here to Bognor for a day or two if necessary. So that relieved me a good deal. I tell you, one can look after oneself all right but this worry about other people who arrive suddenly is about too much!

I am so thankful you are in U. S. but I am constantly haunted by the fear that you may try to get back and by the fear that you are worrying about us. I can't tell you how you need not. We have arranged ourselves as well as possibly can be. But if you were here I should be ill with worry for you—because of the nervous strain, not the danger.

Yesterday I did my chores—anxious the house should be very clean when it faced disaster! Queer how *strongly* one feels that. I put moth powder on all our woollies and tied things up in parcels, tidied everything and saw the meat safe was empty. Told the tradesmen to stop deliveries, took Mr. Pussy to C—— Walk and locked the silver in a cupboard. Then we went off with R. to L—— A—— and on again here last evening. If war comes, I will go back to L—— A——, where I left a suitcase full of jerseys, medicines, books and everything one needs to live for a couple of months.

A. will go to London and join up, staying at O—— Gardens for the day or two which may elapse between registering and being called up. There is four or five days' tinned food there for him. We know how to turn the water off and the gas and light if necessary. It has all been planned at leisure and we know what to do. We took £20 out of the bank in cash. When he is called up I get 17/- a week separation allowance, so I shall be all right. We shan't be able to pay the rent at O——

Gardens. But that will be a pretty general state and I believe dear Mrs. A. will not make trouble, for we are willing to let her sublet it furnished. We can't do anything about it—A. joins up and the chance of making an income is removed and that is that. It doesn't frighten me an atom! Our possessions and responsibilities are so few and light that we can get down to bed rock like this without it worrying us!

His mother, poor lamb, is in a very dangerous position with her money affairs owing to all this crisis and we know what a tough spot Father is in, so we are on our own. And I must say it is more comfortable to be like this and KNOW where one is. I do assure you, you can't know how relieving it is to know where one is and know that 17/- will come in weekly!

Of course there are moments when the whole thing comes over you like a wave of nausea—literally. Or when you feel so low and hopeless you feel you can't talk or think. But the fact that what will happen will happen, and you can only do what is to be done, gets you through, and these times do not last long. So long as one is occupied, one is grand, and I think, too, that personal feeling is rather numbed. I don't think and don't feel much about A. going off. I know he can't do anything else and I know that in a war separation is no harder than being together—in fact, considering the way strain upsets relationships—it is probably *better* for him to go, as far as our happiness is concerned. No doubt I shall feel more about this when it happens, but one has

learnt only to look at the *day's* affairs and not to anticipate feeling.

I haven't been away from my house much so haven't
seen how London takes it. It was very very quiet yesterday. Less people in the streets than usual, less noise,
except of aeroplanes. Many cars loaded up with people
evacuating (like us!) but less than in September—far
less. The trains were quite empty, which surprised us.
Most people are on holiday. The crowds on the front
here are very full of holiday spirit. We heard two people, a girl and a young man, talking on a train yesterday.
He said "What do you think of it all?" She said "Oh, I
dunno, do you think it will come to anything?" and then
they dropped it. The working class don't know much
about it I guess. They will just take it when it comes.

The authorities do seem to have profited by the year's
grace after Munich and I believe preparations for evacuation and air defence etc. are efficient and well thought
out now—we are *ready* for it.

It is nice to be here after the strain of the week and
just let up for 24 hours. I don't take much hope from
the President's gallant peace attempts. I believe Hitler
has got to have this war or lose his face and I believe
we probably can't stall any longer. Anyway I feel perfectly confident *this* time that we are going to see it
through and not make a Munich again. At last we are
behaving with dignity and resolution. What a relief it
is too.

A. has seen that the Hearns understand how to darken

C—— Walk and what room to use as a refuge room—the servants' sitting room. It is excellent for that. And they have a store of food there so Father will be all right.

I do assure you that to be here *in it*, knowing what to do, is much less dangerous and awful than it seems to you over there. Provision is made for the emergency here which you can't know about. It is only this waiting which has been so hard on the nerves.

If you don't hear from me for a while do not worry. The posts are very much held up and between now and Friday next I may be moving to L—— A—— and being pretty busy, and having much to think about.

We are fine, and be damned to Hitler. Tell Americans that we are behaving all right at last!

Heaps of love, darling C., be confident that all is well. *Nothing* can happen to us that really matters—believe this. I do.

SURREY
September 3, 1939

DARLING C.:

Censorship is in and we are told to write clear brief letters to anyone abroad, so you will understand that is why mine won't be so full as usual. This day war was declared but we had felt as if we were at war for the past 2 days—still actual declaration does make it feel rather more *intense*, as it were.

A. is here tonight, he goes home (our house) tomorrow

[47]

and is applying to the regiment he picked out to enlist in right away. I hope they take him, for the sooner he is settled the better and apart from that he hasn't really anywhere to live now except solitarily in our house.

I have spent half today helping with evacuated mothers and children from London, which was as helpful for me as them! It is very easy for someone with a clear head to be pretty useful—anywhere I guess, specially if you aren't shy and don't mind just plunging in and doing whatever appears to need doing. I am going to be able, I rather hope, to find a good deal to do even here, before even the food-growing garden work has to be started. And if that is the case all is O.K. by me. I expect this reminds you of the last war and you!

Really the strain is so much less now than it has been the last two weeks, and it is a kind of relief to be fighting this war. We want to fight it and get it over—get over for always the kind of strain we have been living in ever since Hitler turned up. Even our own married life for instance has been worried and harassed by him —by the constant reminders of what he was doing—we were never at peace.

The censor may be beginning to think this isn't brief enough—one will have to find by trial and error how much he does think brief. Let me know if he lets this through so I will know what is all right!

September 7, 1939

DARLING C.:

Your first letter—for my birthday—arrived while our first raid signal was going at 7:30 A.M. yesterday. A *lovely* morning and no sign of anything. They had actually never reached the coast even, and I must say we felt no alarm. One knows what to do and anyway it was such a pretty morning! Then I had another letter by Dixie Clipper today. I can't tell you how lovely it was to get them. To start with about me. I am here with blessed R. indefinitely, but certainly for the beginning till we know how heavy raids will be. It is in a safe area and I don't intend to go to London at all, so you can be free of worry for me. Our plane detector business is marvellous and though it may be a nuisance to get ready for a raid when the planes are hundreds of miles away, it is a reassuring thing to do and makes one feel well looked after.

I shan't overwork—indeed I am having the easiest time I've had for months for I help with the housework, but with three of us it doesn't take long, and otherwise I am just sitting in the *gorgeous* sunshine in the garden. I did do some work in the village at the beginning but that is over now. And I shall do *something*—but I'm waiting to see what is needed around here and what I can best do. Actually R. and I had planned to come here to raise vegetables and grow as much food as possible and that is what we shall do when the season begins. And

[49]

I hope I shall learn how to bottle and preserve because we'll have heaps more than we can use.

So you see I am awfully well settled. I had worked it all out before and I closed the house and put moth stuff all over *well* in time and got away here before the great rush out of town began. So be absolutely easy about *me*.

Don't, *darling* C., feel you are a deserter. This isn't like the last war. The less people there are here the better they like it. There are *too many* people volunteering for national work. The officials are distracted by them. All the women's services are over full. Though they still want odd wardens here and there, but you *couldn't* do that work. Everything was organized so well ahead this time and the best thing one can do is to make as few demands on anything or anyone as possible and keep out of congested areas where they have to look after you. This is really true. Even the army is plumb full and you have to wait to get in! It is so different from last time when it was all excitement and drama and romance. This war is just a *job*, and has been worked out like any other national business, like pensions or traffic control. I must say I *like* it that way. We don't feel very flag-wagging. It is just a matter of getting rid of Nazis as quickly as possible. Or Nazism, really.

I will try and tell you what has been happening with me. I left Bognor the Monday before the war and came here. A. drove me here from there. R. was in London that day and he and I spent the afternoon darkening this house as quickly as possible. This actually took several days because it is an awkward job and we did it temporarily then with paper. Now R. has got some good special curtains and we are doing it over. It takes quite a time to darken the house every evening and is an awful bore.

That week (lovely weather all the time) was really HELL. A. went away to Bognor and to London, stopping here always on the way. I felt desperately about leaving O— Gardens and the break up of our life—this has been for me and for R. the most horrible thing of all. We listened continuously to the wireless (the BBC has been *magnificent* throughout all this, so steady, human, decent and factual) waiting first for our answers to Hitler and then his answers to us, terrified that Chamberlain would give in again and terrified of war, always hoping for a miracle and knowing it wouldn't happen and always homesick for our houses. (This is a furnished cottage R. and P. have and R. doesn't like the furnishings any better than I do. They are pseudo-tudor!) Also our nerves were getting frayed. I can't remember the days separately at all. It was just one long grim time. Then Friday, when A. was here, he and I sat on the porch and heard the announcer say, "There is grave news today" before even the weather report was given! That was about Germany invading Poland. So we knew it was coming.

That evening before A. went away I reached a kind of climax. I hadn't been sleeping very well and I had five frightful minutes when I thought I would go bug-house. I suddenly realized it was here and there was no way out of it. It was a bad five minutes. There will never be anything worse—a sort of claustrophobia. But I got out of it. I took a lot of long deep breaths very steadily and didn't touch A. at all, and remembered that even in the worst kind of war *Most of the Day* is normal. It isn't a constant heavy cloud. Routine goes on: every-thing looks the same most of the time. It *isn't* really a wall closing one in. When I made myself see this, tak-ing the deep breaths, I began to come, as it were, to the surface. A. was perfect. He stood there saying, *"You'll be all right"* and not trying to help me—which would have been unbearable. That night I went to bed very early and slept like a log. The next day I was absolutely O.K. I went and helped in the village—receiving evacu-ated mothers and children, giving them cups of tea and generally cheering them, and on Sunday, when A. came again, I was again helping with the village. I felt *fine. That* was when war was declared. While I was helping, fifteen minutes after we declared war, A. (who was help-ing too) said, "They have started—the siren went just now." As you will know, it was a false alarm, but we didn't know that then. I was busy and I didn't care. I knew what to do if they actually came over us and I had no fear or worry.

Since then I've been feeling quite different from what I did that awful week. The tension has gone and life *is* normal and I don't think about our house but just put all that out of my mind firmly and cope with what is around. And the wonderful weather helps a lot. R., poor lamb, got her "catharsis" later. She went to London the other day to get some things from B—— Street, saw King's Road all sandbagged, the house in a mess and everything looking rather unnatural. So she had *her* bad five minutes that evening and luckily I had had mine and could help a bit. But ever since *she* has been a different person too—like her old self, instead of strained and nervy.

I tell you all this because I'm sure you want to know how we felt and what it felt like even though it seems very ego-centric to speak of such things. A. went to London finally on Monday and now he *is* in the Army! He got in so delightfully—so like him. I've written you how we both wanted him to—he and me, and why. I hope you understand—anyway conscription is coming in a few days, the Bill is passed already—though of course his age group wouldn't have been called up for a long time. But he's never considered trying to get a noncombatant job and he wanted to get in as soon as possible. This is *his* war (and mine too). Well anyway he wanted to get in a certain regiment (I think I told you which in a pre-war letter and I can't say which now because of the censor!). But they are very closed-up and don't take any old recruit. However, he went along there the day after war was declared and saw the sergeant major who winked and said, "We're all full up and not allowed to take any more but—perhaps . . . Can you drive a car?" A. said,

"Yes, any car." So the S.M. led him to a group of most charming (A. says) officers—all about 30 to 40 years old, with nice smiles and hair greying at the temples. And they grinned at A. and he grinned at them and they said, "I think we must have *lost* the papers you sent in before." They were sweet. And you can see how they would be, with A. looking so darling and happy and confident and modest. So they told him to go back and get his kit and join the regiment that night at their new H.Q. which is outside London.

Actually there was a muddle and he had to go somewhere else to join them in the end, the next day, and meanwhile he fell in with another regiment who were even nicer and very keen for him to come in with them. But he already had esprit de corps or something and stuck to the original lot. But if he wants to later, he can probably transfer. Anyway both were very nice and now he is with the first lot and I am waiting to hear from him and know just what he is. He will join as a ranker of course, but I rather imagine promotions will come to him quickly. I do so love the way he did it—just walking up to a regiment he knew was full but which he had decided on and wanted to be in and *getting in*—as he always does because he bears himself in such a way that people always want him and see what he is. It is a kind of germ of success he always carries in him. He will be, I think, a long time training and I don't look ahead. His being in the army doesn't worry me—it may later, but it doesn't now. It seems so natural and I know he will always be all right. It was *natural* for him to be there and that is what seems important. We do what we *want to do*, then whatever happens we are all right.

What is unnatural is losing our home and home life and that is hard to cope with. But I am just trying to make a life here instead and I *am* too. I am so *lucky* being here with R. We both feel the same way about things and can have such fun together even in these days. And she is fearless, physically, which is a very good thing for me.

I don't see much of the outside world so I can't tell you what it is like. We all carry our gas masks in a box wherever we go. Everyone in the streets has theirs slung over their shoulder. The roads are pitch black at night. No lights, even traffic lights only show a tiny thin red cross of light. Cars are almost entirely lightless—and one just doesn't go on the roads at night if it can possibly be helped. *I* haven't. Rationing hasn't come in yet, though it will in a day or two and there isn't and won't be any shortage. It is being done to avoid profiteering, very wisely. Everyone seems to wear armlets saying what they are working in. In London all men wear them if they belong to a large corporation—P. for instance has B.B.C. on his.

The B.B.C. gives news about every two hours and the programme is only a single one at present—mostly music. We know very little of what is happening at the front except in Poland which is bad, but only as we expected. We are all cheered and delighted by the R.A.F. dropping leaflets.

Father wrote me very cheerfully today and I shall write back. A. went to see him just before he enlisted. J. is in Scotland with P. Everyone being scattered seems a bit gloomy at first, but I feel very sure that this is temporary and when we get into our stride and know how things are going to be we shall get about and see each other and perhaps even re-settle in London. But *not* before we know it is a wise thing to do!

Lunch is ready and I must stop. Heaps and heaps of love. I feel v. cheerful and serene and the thought of you worrying is about my only disquieting *personal* thought. It is so LOVELY to have you there in non-war, normal circumstances. *Write just as often as you can.* You can't think how I love to hear from you.

SURREY
December 16, 1939

DARLING C.:

A. writes that he is sure to get leave for Christmas, perhaps three days and very possibly five days. But I don't know when it begins, though I am supposing that Christmas Day will come into it. We will be in London and are having lunch with Father and supper with the K.'s. Beyond that I don't know what we shall do quite, but I expect we shall pretend to settle down in our house and see whatever people we still know who are

still in London. London is such a dark gloomy place
that I never particularly look forward to being there, but
I notice that when one has spent a day or two there
one gets used to it and it seems quite pleasant. Still I
wouldn't stay there now for anything. Everyone looks
tired and strained—they are all on First Aid posts or ambulance units or something and have to hang around
waiting all night or all day and it certainly tires them
out. And of course it isn't a lot of fun being in London
when you can't afford even to go to the movies—at
least more than once. Oh, this certainly is a queer queer
time. One feels more or less normal down here, specially
now I have my routine teaching Sally and Sue, but one
is certainly getting very stupid and dull. It is like living
in a dream all the time.

A. has been in the west of England for the past two
weeks, and billeted, oddly enough, on an American
family—artisans but very sweet and good to him. He got
good food there too so I guess he will feel pretty sorry
to go back to headquarters. The other night he went
out on a jag with another man from his battery and in
the course of it they met three very nice men. They
were all rather pie-eyed by then and didn't know who
they were, but accepted an invitation to lunch the next
day—luckily they were off duty then. When they turned
up they found them nicely ensconced in the hotel
with drinks waiting for them. They had a most lovely
lunch and talked about America and architecture and
all sorts of nice things which A. said you never talk

about in the army. So that was fun for him. Otherwise it was a rather depressed letter, saying that separation was beginning to make him feel rather frantic, also the international situation—I don't mean the progress of the war, but the new situation with Russia and everyone being so smug about her when they weren't about other places that did just the same thing.

SURREY
January 4, 1940

DARLING C.:

No news at all—we've just sat indoors as near the fire as possible. I haven't seen A. since Xmas but he telephoned me that he is really well, and also that his Major told him that they are doing all they can to push his name forward for a commission. In the usual course of events he couldn't get one for months—owing to his never having been in the O.T.C. [Officers' Training Corps] (at Public School). However I'm not counting on it yet—and even so I feel two ways about it, for it very much increases the possibility of his being sent abroad—and that may be anywhere these days. However it wouldn't happen for some months, so I am just not worrying at all—One doesn't worry ahead these days—I must say it saves strain! We just feel, as K. said so perfectly the other day, "Well, all this isn't what *I* reckoned for." I never heard the war summed up so well for us!

Wasn't Roosevelt's speech *wonderful*—he gets better

all the time—really inspiring, and how bold of him to say it out so straight with all that isolationist vote. Perhaps that means he isn't running for the 3rd term and doesn't care. Anyway it was grand. And do you see how Daladier in his big New Year speech almost openly alluded to Federal Union—and we hear that "influential French opinion" (at least so the wireless said) is talking about it—of course it isn't specifically called that. It makes me quite encouraged—if only we'd foreshadow a few tempting peace terms to the German people and so give them something that made them feel it was worth turning out the Nazis.

SURREY
January 12, 1940

DARLING C.:

There is less and less news here, we only think about the cold lately. It has been the severest winter I can remember. I don't know why I don't mind it more—one does feel cold, and yet it doesn't have that devastating effect on one which I always thought it would have. We have had frost continually now for over a month. Of course it isn't like wretched Berlin, but it seems terrific for England.

A. turned up suddenly for a day last weekend. He is now on duty somewhere and I imagine has actually been doing his stuff from what one gathers of the news this week, so that will be interesting for him. But he is in the most frightful place—in a marsh deep in snow,

[59]

sleeping in a hut, quarter of a mile from any water, which has to be fetched by buckets. He is eight hours on duty and eight hours off—day and night. It must be intolerable, but he says you just get so you don't mind. It is simply something to get through. He is a marvel . . . After he described this frightful place—so ugly too, and pretty unattractive companions, he said in his letter, "Don't think I am depressed by this place. I am sure I can make something of it." It makes one undepressed oneself to have him say such things, bless him.

Last night R. and I put on the gramophone and heard the whole of the Schumann Carnaval, Rachmaninoff playing it. I remember you thought that he wasn't so good after the first piece, but I must say when one hears it all it seems pretty grand, although in one or two of the frivolous parts he is a little Russian and heavy handed. The B.B.C. have been running a series called "Make your own Music," rather sweet, telling people who are, like us, evacuated from cities and living alone in the country, how to get together and make little orchestras or even, if you are solitary, how to get fun out of a piano or gramophone when you don't know how to play or listen. Darling Walford Davies told how it was fun to put on an orchestral record and then sit down at the piano and accompany it with one finger, picking out the melody. One always thinks one will do these things, and R. and I mean to play duets a lot but somehow there is very little time. It is so odd how music has become so important—it is always there and even if one does nothing about it, it is still there for one, which is so comforting and good. I expect you have heard of Myra Hess's project—she runs concerts in the National Gallery at a shilling a seat at lunch time. They are so crowded out that there are queues and they have started extra ones at tea time.

SURREY
January 26, 1940

DARLING C.:

Even yet I don't see how it would have been better for you to come here when the war began, or before. We expected terrible things: one's only thought was to get away and get everyone away. I only had happiness in thinking of you over there, away from it. And even now we have no reason to suppose that this country is a good place to come to. If we decide to take steps to get on with the war (and so, I suppose, end it sooner, perhaps, if more unpleasantly) it may be not at all a good place to be in and I'll feel as desperately as ever that I want you there. It isn't just a matter of safety. It is of the greatest importance to us all that some people should remain in full possession of a kind of pre-war sanity, not muddled and bored and dérangé like us. Not, I mean, in order to regulate the world, but just so we can restore ourselves by getting back our old balance from them, serenity and so on.

Of course the way you are feeling now doesn't make you feel you are being very sane either. And all the time

[61]

I've felt you had the right to be here when you wanted to be and that however much relief it gave us to feel you were in safety and comparative serenity, we hadn't the right to try to keep you away from your own people, or from where you wanted to be.

If A. gets transferred and eventually goes to France he thinks I ought to go to U. S. for a while (I don't know where the passage money would come from). And if we should have a baby he is sure I should. I think so too, in the latter case. It is unlikely we will—I know the idea would strike you as crazy. But I can't tell you what an urge there is to it—I suppose Nature doing her stuff about keeping up the population really—but one feels oneself that since one's home has been broken up, and life with one's husband, that one yearns to do something that will extend it, keep it alive somehow, and a baby, I suppose, is the only thing. It is like defying the out-side forces, or something—they *won't* break us up like that.

I'm just back from town—A. had 48 hours' leave. We were at our house—perhaps our last stay there together, for if it doesn't get let in a week or so, it goes back to the landlady, who has a chance to let it unfurnished. You know it has been phenomenally cold this winter with a long protracted frost, (though no wind, thank heaven)—of course the pipes were frozen so we had to get pails of water from the neighbours to wash in, even to use the W.C.! But we adored being there—it was so short—each time leave seems shorter and shorter. But we had dinner in the dining room with two candles in tarnished silver candlesticks, for the first time since the war, and had breakfast in bed, and talked and went out to the theatre and enjoyed ourselves generally. Where A. has been it has been intensely cold (for England—12 below zero) and he is in a marshy wet place, sleeping in a wooden hut—somehow he sails over these discomforts —more than discomforts really—and the monotony of the life. In his hours off duty he translates Flaubert! No news of a commission yet, though his C.O. said he hoped it would come through in a few weeks. But they are giving commissions to all the 19-year-old O.T.C. lads before they even consider men who haven't had O.T.C. training, however able they are at their jobs.

On Wednesday, after A. left at lunch time, I lunched with Mrs. R. and my friend Margery M. whom I hadn't seen since before the war—great fun. Then we all went to a debate on Federal Union. Then I went to a Warburg lecture—first since the war—what a relief to hear something so good and decent and abstract and full of fine scholarship. Then to C—— Walk where Father and I had a nice cosy little dinner before going to the G.'s party—the first big party given since the war. I must say it was rather fun and I saw a lot of old faces and felt cheered by seeing them. Father hadn't been out after 6 P.M. since the war and was full of fears—it is perfectly easy to get about specially when, like him, you take taxis. And there was a full moon (all parties are planned for full moons) so the streets were as clear as daylight. The moon lights everything up much better now there is very little street lighting. So it was all very simple and easy, though poor father kept trying to make me leave, from 10:30 on, because he was SURE there would be no taxis! However as it was my first and perhaps my last chance (anyway for an unforeseeable time) of seeing people I managed to keep on there till 11:30! I stayed that night at C—— Walk and the next day looked up the Federal Union headquarters to get some material with which to start a branch here, which I feel I must at least *try* to do. It is the only hope, even if the plan has got to be modified a good deal before it can be applied. It is surprising how many people are beginning to allude to it in public speeches—including of course Daladier—though they don't allude to it by name. And this complete union we have with France is a wonderful beginning for it.

I start giving lessons to Sally and the "paying pupil" next week. There is a slight thaw so we hope this long spell of cold is breaking up. I haven't found it intolerable, though it has been wearing and I think has taken away one's resilience of spirits. One feels very bogged in this war—shut in and shut off—there is nothing to look forward to and that gives you a bad feeling sometimes. But life here is just as nice as it can be under the circumstances—we somehow reap a lot of fun from it. The only thing that is wrong with it really is that it is unnatural, so you can never feel yourself—I expect that is rather how you feel too—de-functionalized. However it *will end* sometime.

SURREY
February 16, 1940

DARLING C.:

While he was on leave, A. and I went to a Warburg lecture—so lovely, all about Bernini and the conflict between him and French academic art of the 17th century—a beautifully "removed" subject and new to us. We did enjoy it. Saw several friends there. Then we dined with the C.'s. A. C. was sweet and he and A. did a lot of soldiers' talk together. In spite of being bored in the army (they call it "browned up" in the army— fed up with the waste of time, red tape, the feeling of being caught and no escape, being in a machine—all that, and you'll understand) A. is awfully interested in it, interested in good soldiering and how it is done and the distinction between good and professional soldiers and civilian amateur ones. I'm beginning to catch from him a great deal of respect for the professional army man, who is no fool evidently. So talking to an old soldier like A. C. gives him great pleasure. Anyway, to get back to dinner—this was *delightful*; so lovely to be in that house again, with wine and spirits flowing freely and see high ceilings and lovely curtains. And to be able to talk to E. and say all I wanted to, however boring it was. Also we went to a show of Hitchens' pictures.

[65]

They are magnificent now. You know he has really "arrived." Critics constantly commend him. Now, I suppose, it is too late, though I believe the picture market isn't as dead as one would think.

We had drinks with J. and S. one day. J. also just recovered from flu; S. had it two weeks ago and now quite well. Incidentally he has been finally rejected for the army. You know they have done the most heroic thing. Taken that tragic refugee woman into their house. You'll have heard about her. It is a thing I couldn't do, and I have the greatest admiration for J. for doing it—even though she says she couldn't *not* do it. The woman, though magnificently courageous (the day we saw her she behaved with such quiet gaiety and dignity) can't keep it up—the whole behaviour collapses—she has delusions, sees the scenes all over again, thinks her husband is coming into the room insane, thinks the Germans are right there—it is hideous, poor poor thing. As J. says, it is impossible to comfort her because you can hold out no hope. The only news that can help would be that her husband was dead—that would give her hope of being happy *some* time. But they may never hear anything. They hope she will move into a flat they have found for her now. But that won't mean they don't have some responsibility for her, for she relies on them when these times come on her—usually at night. So that is as good a piece of war work as I have heard of.

T. rang me up. She has just had news that her family in Poland is alive. That is all she knows. She sounded frantic and says life has been terrible. One can't do anything.

Well this all sounds pretty bad. It throws our own condition into a good light though. We have been so lucky—so well looked after. This has been a bad month morally—I think because of the long cold weather which weakened our mental resistance and of course the news hasn't been very uplifting—Poland and Finland and the slaughter at sea. Don't let anyone say that this war is "queer" or a "no-war." It is only in one place that there isn't activity—and that is the Maginot Line. But there is a war at sea like nothing we have ever known or heard of and I think it's outrageous that people overlook it.

However, with the warmer weather I think we'll all come back to life again a little. And also no doubt we are going through that transition stage of getting over the drama of the beginning of the war and settling down to the possibility of a long and tedious siege of it. Perhaps too, it won't be so long. I shouldn't go to news reels at the movies. I saw some of Finland and it was upsetting.

We are dismantling the house as soon as A. gets his next leave, perhaps next week. We couldn't let it furnished and the landlady is taking it back—not a word, bless her, about the unpaid rent for 6 months. I dare say, when the war ends, we may well get it back if we want it, for I rather think the new tenants don't want a long lease. Now the point has come I don't feel badly about it. I felt awful at first, but we have been expecting this so long that I am quite used to the idea of losing it and somehow quite hardened about it. The responsibility of having it and not being able to pay and also the thought of it gradually deteriorating, the furniture I mean—in dust and disuse makes it easier to give it up. So I don't feel badly now at all. Anyway you can't feel bad about what is inevitable. If there is no alternative to something you just do it and that is that. The chief bore is having nowhere to go that is ours when A. has leave, and always having to hope for offers of beds and dinners. However we always have made out and I don't doubt that we always will, and people have been angelic to us and so generous and kind.

SURREY

March 1, 1940

DARLING C.:

On the last afternoon of A.'s leave we had a lovely afternoon. We had £3 deposit for the Electricity Co. back, so A. made me go and buy a hat and shoes and silk stockings (which I didn't need but they were cheap) and a new neck handkerchief. We went along Oxford Street together looking at things and feeling terribly gay and happy. It was fun to have a hat and shoes— good pretty ones—and he was so sweet about it and gay. And then we went to the movies and had sherry with E. and went to dinner at Simpson's and had a drink with J. G. (by accident) at the Café Royal. Then we parted and A. went back to the barracks. Rather awful to lose him after a whole fortnight together. Longer than any time since the war, and heavenly. I used to be afraid that when we hadn't a home it would upset and un- settle us—the house meant so much in our life together. But I can see now it isn't going to. We've got some- thing far more permanent and solid even than a house —though I wouldn't like not to have one *just as soon as we can* again, when peace comes. And he says we will and he says we are going to be all right. He had one of his funny "visions"—I mean queer—about what was go- ing to happen to us and it *was all right.*

He had it, or told me it, just before he left and a good thing he did, because that night, which I spent at C—— Walk, a siren went off at 4:30 and we (Father and I in the study and the Hearns downstairs) spent two hours waiting for guns to go off before we found that it was a mistake—some siren went off in error just across the river. It wasn't much fun and it made me glad again that you weren't there. Actually one doesn't need to get excited till one hears guns close by, so I knew all along that nothing dangerous was happening and might never happen, but still waiting is rather exhausting and dread- ful. I sat in the study with Father, he snoozing all the time, and I trying to read and every now and then thinking "in half an hour I may not be here" which made me feel not very nice. About every fifteen minutes I went down and looked out at the street, and imagined

I heard aeroplanes. In the end, in waiting, you don't know whether you want something to happen to break up the suspense, or are glad that at least so much time has gone by and you are still there to know it.

I took an early train to get back here in time for lessons so I never went back to bed. It was my first experience of a "raid"—the sirens went off here once or twice at the beginning of the war but you don't feel it the same way in the country, and they were more subdued anyway.

I am back to routine now after this fortnight's gay time. The snow and frost are over thank goodness and now there are just the usual March winds which are also cold but more hopeful, and the spring flowers are coming up, but not the vegetables, which were all killed by the frost—rather serious.

I feel that about May I shall begin to take stock of my situation and think of something else to do. I really must get a real job for we have now only £5 in the bank. But now the winter is over everything seems clearer and more normal and nothing seems so impossible. Anyway, what a marvellous time we all have coming to us—and what a good thing to have this war *behind* us instead in front of us as it has been ever since I grew up. It makes one feel quite cheerful to think of that!

SURREY

March 5, 1940

DARLING C.:

I know so well what is eating you—the feeling you aren't *anywhere* and not relevant and that even here you wouldn't have a place. It is so stoopid to try and say things that just sound comforting, but here are some things which are true which might make you feel better. To start with you aren't alone in being placeless and in feeling irrelevant—if you were here you would find that is true—you are just like one of the rest of us; you happen to be in Florida, I happen to be in Surrey. And here, hundreds and hundreds of women, not only working-class ones, are pushed off away from their homes and husbands in the country and just left to feel no use and as if they were deserting people and not helping anyone. If this sounds as if I were being reproachful it is an absolute mistake and due to the way I am saying it. I just mean that it makes me feel as if you were one of us, in the same plight, for the same reasons, and it kind of joins you up with us instead of separating us—we're all evacuees or refugees or something. *That* is what this particular war has meant to us.

SURREY

March 9 or 10, 1940

DARLING C.:

I was in town last week for a night because A. was able to come up for an afternoon and we both went to a

[71]

Warburg lecture by Summerson on Corbusier, so you see life has moments of normality still and I think they will increase now. Specially now the winter is over, we are all feeling more like human beings and beginning to look around and see whether we need really to feel so cut off from everyone. One result of this was that I wrote to Mrs. S. and then went over to see her on Sunday—it only takes as long to get there as it does to get to Hampstead from Chelsea, in spite of having to bike to the station, take a train, take a bus and then walk a mile! She was so happy to see me and I her too, more specially since I saw A. and C. who were up from Wales for a rare weekend. They are absolutely there now and feel very cut off. A. has 12 evacuated children and two teachers—she had 17 at the beginning of the war. She hoped for real slum children that you could build up and help but of course got some from the petit bourgeois refined suburban areas of B——! She says they have all been sent nightdress cases from home made like giant pandas. (Some, anyway.) We had a great long talk together of the war and how we all felt about everything and agreed with great feeling.

SURREY
March 19, 1940

DARLING DARLING C.:

Well, spring really has come, though the weather is very unsettled, but no longer cold. The trees are still black but the crocuses are well out and the grape hya-

cinths, and things look human again. Of course everything is late—so of course Easter is early, but still it isn't
quite the holiday it used to be! Though A. *is* getting
four days' leave, but I guess will have to spend most of
it with his poor mother who is awfully sad and upset,
poor dear.

I feel I have written so grumblingly about the past
winter and our various troubles—you know nothing was
so bad really: or the bad times always passed over
quickly. Now the house has gone, I really don't feel anything about it—perhaps because I am not there to see
it and life has altered so much that one can't feel it or
compare things. I've been so *lucky* having a place to live
and having A. in England and seeing him so often. That
is all that matters—I live from day to day and there are
so many very pleasant things in the days.

P. has just had 3 days' leave. He was cheerful, cynical,
worried and serene. He said we were in for some bad
times now. He also told us when he thought the war
might be over. I won't say when it was, out of supersti-
tion, but it was a term we can all bear. Just having a
term set to it makes me feel *grand*. Of course unforeseen
things occur and no one can know. But *still*—none of us
want any peace *now*; it would amount to losing the war
and would mean years of horror, worse than 1933 to
1939, waiting for the next outbreak from Germany. Nobody wants it—not even for the sake of having homes
again and seeing husbands and having a few months'
peace. It would be no good. So whatever Musso. and

[73]

Hitler are cooking up there in Rome it won't come to anything.

I saw A. last weekend. He got Saturday afternoon off and I went up to London and we both went to J. G.'s wedding reception. A. was the only man in uniform there! That means nothing, but it surprised us. Of course our contemporaries haven't been called up yet, so it is natural too. It was fun going to a wedding reception and we drank a lot of champagne and after had dinner with the C.'s which was nice. A. C. and A. sit forever over brandy discussing the army like two old veterans.

Next day I went up to A.'s depot and saw him just at lunch time which we had in a pub close by. The headquarters are in a largeish Edwardian country house and the wooden huts for stores, eating places etc. are all over the grounds. A.'s billets are in some new empty houses (so DAMP) about a ¼ mile away from H.Q. It was interesting seeing where he spends most of his life now, though of course I wasn't allowed in the H.Q. grounds or billets. A man who had been in the ranks with A., but now had a commission, came into the pub with his wife while we were there and it was amusing to see A. and him just chatting away, no saluting or formality. They came and sat beside us later. A nice young man who got his commission at once because he had his Certificate A. from his O.T.C. All the O.T.C. men got commissions automatically, after a week or two in the ranks without any question of suitability. But if you weren't in the O.T.C. you have to wait forever—like A.

who is obviously excellent officer material. However being in the ranks has kept him in England so I am not
grumbling.

SURREY
March 28, 1940

DARLING C.:

I shouldn't get overworried by the pessimistic outlook
of American press people, even though they are well-in-
formed like Elmer Davis. You see, the apparent prospects so often seem ominous—every *fact* one can lay
hands on seems to add up to something bad: and yet
that isn't quite all the truth or the whole of the situation. For one thing, it seems as if only the ominous facts
were the ones which were made available to the public.
Germany seems to have made a greater effort at publiciz-
ing her assets than we have and also the outside world
must judge our capacity a good deal from the mentality
and past records of our statesmen, which (if the censor
will allow me) I will say, mildly, isn't much to go on. But
what we will run this war on is the capacity of our men
of action and research, our specialists and real workers
behind the scenes—and that you don't and can't hear
about. In the things that matter—in fact, in the things
that make for winning a campaign, economic or military
—there is a lot more to us than meets the eye, I think.
Of course it might be better if we had younger and more
elastic-minded people at the top; the clever people could
then get their way without so much obstruction and need

for slow explanation. But still there it is—and we can't talk about it. Germany is trying to bluff even yet and if she can persuade everyone else that she holds all the tricks, of course it has an effect indirectly on her enemy. You can't trace the ways in which she convinces neutral opinion that she has got it her own way, but if a man like Davis is pessimistic it is because she is putting her stuff over. Look how the U. S. papers were taken in by the German version of the Sylt affair. Perhaps even it will seem to you that I am equally taken in by the British version. I am prepared to think that Sylt isn't wiped out, but it is also clear to see that it was a big job and effectively carried out. You see—we didn't claim to wipe it out: we were specific and undramatic in stating the facts and one can draw one's own conclusions if one reads the reports carefully.

Goodness, I sound like the Ministry of Information trying to put over propaganda—what a stoopid thing to be doing to you. But I just wanted to say—be reassured. America can only know what the belligerents choose to tell her and that is probably very little in the end, and the outsider always sees a much more complicated, long-drawn-out affair than we do. I do think we are in for a worrying time, but it isn't like last September—or like Munich. We haven't got a war to come. P. says there's not a shadow of doubt that we'll win: it's just a question of struggling through the preliminary unpleasantness! And that may not be so easy. But don't you worry. Just think of what our Air Force has done—and it so much smaller than the German one—the alertness and ingenuity and real thoroughness with which they've carried out so many jobs all the time and all at the same time. Yet before the war, we felt the German Air Force was overwhelming. That's the kind of thing I mean when I say that people can't judge by just the concrete facts available to them.

SURREY

April 1, 1940

DARLING C.:

It *is* hard not to have lowered feelings about the war, and what use is it. The alternative is to think of peace, at present. It would be impossible to live in. So we just have to have war. Had people been wiser we need never have had one—but one has to go back ten years to repair that damage, so that's no use to think of.

P. still maintains his stand on the limit he put to the war—if he is right, we can all stand it. Sometimes I feel dreadfully when I think what I am losing, and do dread being old and faded when it is over—and we not hardly married yet. But mostly I don't: determination is all one is left with, so I suppose it gives one satisfaction to feel it. A. feels rather helpless and hopeless about his commission. His C.O. told him he didn't like losing his best men by their getting commissioned and A. suspects that he isn't trying to do anything towards getting A.'s application through. It's a kind of waste of time for A. to

spend so many hours washing dishes and sweeping billets—which is mainly what a private's life consists of.
Still, there it is. And he *is* in England.

April 15, 1940

DARLING C.:

Well, aren't the navy being lovely? Or don't you hear
so much about it? It has pepped us all up a lot and everyone is so delighted that the Nazis have tried to burst out,
for it shows they are getting desperate. And now we have
all the Norwegian shipping (the 3rd largest Mercantile
Marine in the world) and no beastly neutrality to bother
about.

Of course we know it won't be all jam from now on.
Perhaps by the time you get this the Nazis will be in
Holland and then I suppose they will fly over us a bit.
But this is just what we are ready for and will give us a
chance to get back at them. So don't on my account be
worried if you hear how near the war is getting to us, for
till something like that happens and things begin to
shoot, we can't see the end properly in sight. Perhaps
by then Italy will be in too, and although it's gloomy to
have another enemy, a good many people—and, I believe, all the French—feel that Italy is far less dangerous
as an enemy than as Germany's non-belligerent friend,
because she can get away with murder now and we can't
stop her; whereas she is pretty vulnerable as an enemy

and we could put an end to supplies to Germany coming through her. But what I feel chiefly about *her* is that if she isn't involved in the defeat, she will be a very awkward customer in the peace. It will be very difficult indeed to cope with rebuilding the world if we have one whole fascist country still at large and able to carry on the fascist tradition without interference. I hope this all passes the censor. I don't know if they like such expressions of opinion to be circulated abroad!

So don't get worried about us even if the most sensational things seem to be happening. The past six months has given us time to get ready for anything, the general temper is that we want things to get a move on. Nerves have quietened down since September and the great thing now is not to let the war get boring, so people begin to wonder what the point of being at war is, when nothing is done.

You'll know I am not bloodthirsty, but I feel it is vital that the war finishes as soon as it can, for the sake of the rebuilding afterwards. And if Germany gets going, there's a chance that it can be finished before everyone is ruined or killed. The naval actions of Norway and in Norway have made *all* the difference as to how people feel. A. writes that even at his barracks people feel pepped up and keener.

He is off on his "site" again for six weeks in the country. There has been a great mix-up in his regiment and there is a new colonel so perhaps promotions will be a bit more fairly distributed now. He seems to think his battery will be cleaned up a lot and improved. So that is a good thing because, as I wrote you, he was getting rather fed up with it.

SURREY
May 15, 1940

DARLING C.:

I expect you are feeling worried and there is nothing I can say that will be convincing about the situation not being bad. I can only tell you that we have a feeling that at last we are getting down to it and that everyone feels that they can take what is coming. The day Hitler went in Holland was horrible—I was woken up by the news and it felt a bit like the declaration of war all over again (only worse perhaps)—the same sinking in the stomach, and tremblyness at the knees. It was the most heavenly day—clear hot sun—like it has been all this early summer —and that seemed to make it worse. It was hard teaching the children that day—I couldn't bear to hear aeroplanes which are over us more than ever now—one didn't feel one knew whose planes they might be. I did really expect air invasion that very day. And of course we have heard the guns on the coast all the time lately—it's a rather heartening sound too, which is surprising. A continuous dull booming—our first real noise of war here.

It was a queer strained day—whenever one stopped working, one felt queer and disturbed again. Now we are getting used to it again and used to not very good news. We know we will really get air raids soon now of course.

But the great thing is, this all means the end is nearer—
there never could be an end till the war began and now
it *has* begun—I mean actively, militarily. There has been
a war on all right, as far as we are concerned here at
home, just every minute since Sept. 3. But it wasn't a
war that was getting us nearer the climax.

I have never seen such a beautiful summer in England
or anywhere before. The hedges and ditches really are
lush—the grass so deep and thick and all the hedgeflowers
growing in a kind of profusion I have never seen—wild
parsley feet high, and ground ivy and campion and lady-
smock and of course heaps and heaps of bluebells and
buttercups. All this following on the loveliest month of
apple and pear blossom. It is extravagantly beautiful, and
every day this hot sun and high deep blue sky. I don't
know whether I like it or not—now, after this news, I
think it feels a bit awful.

But of course the great news is Chamberlain's exit.
That was exciting. R. and I listened to the Commons
debate result on the radio—on the Norway campaign—
and when the result of the vote came out with that
ignominious government majority we almost danced. But
even so, I didn't suppose he'd go. The day after Churchill
came in there really was a new feeling in the air. In spite
of bad news, everyone seemed to be drawing a deep
breath, as though they at last hoped to be able to *live*—
it was a kind of release. And his Cabinet is on the whole
so awfully good—splendid about Morrison being at Supply—though there are one or two rather horrible hang-

overs from the old bad days, but I suppose just to conciliate the followers of the old gang. (I hope this passes the Censor.)

I can't tell you what new spirit this change has put into us all, even though we feel pretty grim and desperate— but it isn't an unhealthy desperation—more a kind of business-like feeling.

We are sitting in the garden nearly all the time and the grass has to be mowed continuously which makes a nice smell.

Sue [aged 4]—who is so brown and adorable in her summer frocks—has views on Hitler. She goes into a kind of grumble every now and then, in her low voice, "That old Hitler, that old horrible Hitler, I'll put him on the ash heap."

Really don't worry; this is going to be ALL RIGHT. We know what we are doing and we can take anything because we know it isn't unbearable considering what is going to come out of it. The end of the war is getting nearer.

Cable to same, May 26th.

    A. INSISTS I SAIL ROOSEVELT JUNE FIRST.

THE OFFICIAL'S WIFE

The "B." to whom the rest of the letters in this section are written is the writer of the previous letters. This next batch is written by the woman who was her hostess when she became a "war refugee" in the country. On the outbreak of war "R." went to her week-end cottage, taking her four-year-old daughter Sue. Her husband, "P.," remained in London, where he was doing important official work.

Here is an example of a city woman throwing herself entirely into house and country work, putting behind her all the interests and diversions which had built up her life. In this case, as in the previous letters, the strain of separation from husband and friends can be seen here and there.

"K." is the neighbour in the next house.

SURREY
May 30, 1940

DARLING B.:

I wanted to send you a telegram but was utterly put out by the P.O. officials who declared that my wire might have to be taken out in a rowing boat to the *Roosevelt* by some Irish pirate who would then extort unknown

[83]

sums from yourself. The horrid picture of a departing B. being rooked of her last pennies by some haggling neutral fisherman was more than I could bear. Only I do hope your last moments are not too hideously gloomy.

Well, the week's diary—About Leopold you know, and I won't comment. Though M., who looked in here yesterday and drank gallons of tea on the lawn, had plenty to say as you can imagine. His accounts of things in France were pretty vivid, but as he said with happy smiles, "the higher Hitler climbs, the farther he has to fall."

Horrible things have happened in the garden. Two ringdoves are nesting in the orchard hedge and a litter of baby rabbits is somewhere in the orchard and has eaten *all the stocks*—we've called in the rosy-faced Mr. Street to scythe down the orchard and Strudwick is saving two cartridges from the parachutists to shoot the doves—if we don't carry out these Nazi plans we just won't have any young plants at all. Strudwick and I have had two terrific days among the vegetables, sowing seeds, hoeing, digging, planting potatoes and tomatoes, sticking peas and never stopping exchanging platitudes about Good and Evil and how the latter can't come out of the former etc., etc.

What do you think of the Russian attempt to snub us over Sir S. Cripps' mission? Touchy brutes—or are they truly just vindictive? I must say, an air of spinsterish bridling is rather ludicrous after Finland. If Stalin is go-

ing to behave like an accosted virgin and Mussolini keep
on boasting about a virility which he daren't put to the
test, I really feel they might unload their neuros on one
another and shut their respective traps.

How incredibly, undeservedly lucky we are to have
none of our respective families in Flanders. Guns going
all the week, very soft and one *big* boom at about 6 tonight. The noise seemed to pass overhead and echo back
with two loud cracks, like a whip cracking, from the hills.
Sue thought this GRAND and said "Pop!" admiringly.

June 3, 1940

DARLING B.:

I got your letter from the Shelbourne (opened by the
Censor) this morning, together with a most heartrending
one from W. B.'s stepmother, full of terrible unhappiness
but great pride in him—you know he was in command of
a destroyer, killed at Namsos. So it was rather a sad breakfast, though I was so glad to hear from you. I could just
imagine the desolation of being in Dublin now and it is
good thing to think that by now you've passed through
all those grim antechambers to departure and are really
on your way.

My dear, it is the most perfect type of June day, hot,
hot, hot, and I've just finished distempering [calcimin-
ing] the kitchen, so I too am hot. P. went off to Paris
by plane with X. [a high official] yesterday and returns tomorrow. He sounded so tired on the telephone, but cheer-

[85]

ful and says X. is perfect to work with, intelligent, sensible, open to new ideas and courageous.

M. turned up again with a hollow-faced officer friend, rather grim but very nice, just back with the B.E.F., who suddenly burst out—"I've never been to Germany, I can't speak a word of their bloody language—" and then stopped. It was obvious he could have sworn for hours—and this NOT a Blimp. It was just the things he'd seen; you could see he wanted to be sick and get it out of him. M.'s batman had found a dying girl—machine-gunned—stayed with her till she died, and got lost, and turned up later, to M.'s great delight, at Boulogne (in the early days!). M. looked at our vegetables with GROANS of rage and envy.

R. was here this weekend and we had some good laughs—mostly over the office but also over Il Duce, who R. declares, is NEURO, in fact she maintains he is dying to be stopped coming into the war and leans further and further over in the frantic hope that people will want to stop him. But No, nobody cares now, so PLOP he will soon go with a loud Neuro shriek (disguised as a battle cry), into the abyss.

K.'s girl friend has sent her a preposterous and enchanting gardening hat in which she looks more like Meg in *Little Women* than ever—a flat green straw plate with a red rose plumb on top and green ribbons under her chin, ridiculous and darling. We went into R—— together and found it utterly embattled, signposts gone, strange devices for blocking the roads, all the population standing at the level crossing to wave to troop trains. I may say that our little bridge is not only numbered, but guarded after a certain hour at night by sentries. Mrs. B. [the cook], coming back late from her Sunday evening off, was suddenly challenged to produce her identity card and arrived home almost destroyed by giggles.

I've made all sorts of jam since you went—the last was *seedless* gooseberry from our own green gooseberries; one of those historical recipes from an old Scottish border lady, involving fantastic labours with a teaspoon handle extracting the seeds. One sees well that such grand old housewives had battalions of sweated labour in the shape of 3rd kitchen maids.

Sue has just demanded furiously, "How would you like to have an A.R.P. pin sticking into your shoes?"—True, she has got a drawing-pin in the sole, but A.R.P. pin I suppose it will always be to her! *

How I wish you could see a field of clover near here just now—a broad blazing purple. War is bringing a bit of good cultivation to this countryside for the first time.

Continued June 5th

As you'll see by the date of this, P. just got to Paris in time for the air raid. Quite good aim for such high flying. They got part of the Citroen works, the Air Ministry

* Drawing-pins ("thumb tacks") were used a good deal to fasten black paper and other black-out material to the windows and such preparations were known in home idiom as "A.R.P.," i.e. Air Raid Precautions.

and a nice line of holes across Le Bourget Aerodrome; just enough runway for P. and X. to take off next day with their escort of 4 fighters! P. was tickled to death because he very nearly failed to be in time for the plane—an ancient Provençal taxidriver stopped at each hole to take a decco at it, and exchange blasphemies with other on-lookers. Each time a gendarme would spring forward and demand to know all about P. Long explanations from taxidriver—"My God, this gentleman travels with his Excellency, are we to be detained all day?" Next hole, same performance da capo and P. frantic lest he fail to make Le Bourget. They flew very low to avoid stray Germans, who are rather free with their attentions in the upper air, and P. was sick for the first time, also left his reading glasses in the plane, and when his secretary rang up Croydon about them, she heard they'd gone off in the same plane (it was a bomber) over Germany. Those glasses have always been strayers. By terrific luck, Sue and I had gone over to see Dad for the day and P. had taken two hours off to see his family and walked into the house while we were there. It was marvellous. He immediately tore off his uniform, or most of it (yes, he was back in the old fancy dress) and lay down on the lawn in his Cleopatra position and went to sleep, while we sat round like vultures, waiting for news of Paris, etc. On waking, he had a terrific bout of telephoning and then said he could come back home for the night if I could get him to London by 8 next morning. We had a heavenly eve-ning and a lovely drive early this morning. The place was so lovely and we walked in the orchard till the stars came out.

For three days, Mrs. B. and I have been making hay in the orchard. I wish you could have been here to help, it smelt so good and looks enchanting and, as Mrs. B. says, the haystack will be a grand place for us all to dive into if the Germans turn up!

Wasn't Churchill's speech *great?* There's no news of a distant but very pleasant cousin of R.'s in the 60th Rifles —they were at Calais so I can't believe there's any hope— or of T. N. who'd rejoined his old Regiment, who lost a lot at, I believe, Boulogne.

I've distempered [calcimined] the passage and it smells heavenly. K. was out selling flags for the Red Cross this morning and not one person refused her.

Oh, B., I wish you could see the Seven Stars these days —or just above it, where there's some sort of electrical whatnot. On one side of the road are two soldiers—no, Civil Defence Volunteers—with what *look* like fixed bayonets. On the other side, in the garage of the old lady who smiles at Sue, are two more, reading in deck chairs —War and Peace, in fact. They guard the Elec. Whatnot in relays from 9 P.M. to 6 A.M.

SURREY
June 11, 1940

DEAREST B.:

I just can't believe your farm hasn't been hot when here we have had week after week of magnificent sun and warmth, only broken this week by a few thundery showers out of a glorious blue, windy sky. The kitchen garden is really a sublime sight and we have had peas and beans and peas and beans, till we're blown out with wind like a barrage balloon. I've made jam day after day—raspberry and black currant and white currant and cherry and strawberry (a glut of these and the Govt. gave extra sugar for bought fruit) till my arm ached with stirring and I feel I can never cut the topknot off another black currant as long as I live. I wish you were here to eat the cherry jam which is quite the most ritzy, pre-war, Fortnum and Mason at their best, affair imaginable, entirely stoneless and a deep Imperial purple.

How grand that A. got his stripe, but Oh, dear, how sad that you can't celebrate together. I do hope he gets less labour and more sleep now. It's odd that you should mention A.'s wanting some sort of dynamic counter-propaganda to the Nazi's because P. was saying just the same thing to me the other day. His idea is that our stand is, and must be, more and more the Liberté, Egalité, Fraternité discarded by the French in such a revealing (and almost prophetic) way. He is certain that we will only finally defeat the Nazis by linking up with these submerged principles in Nazi-controlled countries and Germany itself. It's such an un-simple war (as France showed with devastating clearness) and decent people oppose the Nazis for so many different reasons that it's damnably difficult, almost impossible, to find a common slogan. Churchill, Cripps, Wilkinson, Amery, Bevin, Sin-

clair—you'd think the diversity made it easier, but not a
bit. Personally, hearth and home and freedom will do
for me any day and I've a sort of Blimpish disdain for
anybody who wants more! Oh, how you *wouldn't* like
me just now. I've given rein to all the jingo sentiments
in my heart and just mumble Shakespeare to myself and
feel happy to think that England all by herself (except
for the Empire and WHY NOT) is going to win the war
and save the whole world. But, B., in spite of A. and P.
and A.'s soldiers, I can assure you that many many ordinary people feel as I do, and are neither too cynical nor
too self-conscious to feel proud of England. And it's
quite amazing—I could never have imagined it—how
happy it makes me and how I can enjoy every minute of
each day more intensely than ever before. Like being in
love, but more restful.

Well, my dear, after these heroics, I must climb down
a bit and admit that I feel a chill of intense depression
at the thought that K. and the children are probably going next week to America. I don't honestly know what
I'll do without all that cheerful neighbourhood life. Sue,
poor darling, fortunately has no anticipation of what
it'll mean to her. I feel half inclined to send her to the
evacuated school in Gloucestershire, though I hate the
idea of her being away from me in possible air raids. P.
did talk vaguely about sending her to S. Africa; but, B.,
what *is* the use of sending anyone anywhere in the world
today? If things were bad enough to make *here* unsafe,

I'd feel the whole world, not just England, was going up in flames and I couldn't risk her being ill 2,000 miles away from me. And now that I see P. fairly often and he has said outright that he lives for his visits here, I couldn't conceivably leave England, even if the very idea of doing it didn't kill me. No, I think we must accept the gamble for Sue. Nearly everyone I know, incidentally, is in a state of frantic indecision about their children.

June 13, 1940

DARLING B.:

Another week has gone, a rather grim one, with the Germans going all out for Paris and at last, at *last*, Mussolini taking the plunge (one cannot help feeling with a good strong kick in the behind to help him at the last moment). The weather has been strange, at first it was oven-hot and glared, but on Sunday there were false thunderstorms that came to nothing, and on Monday it was black and awful, and ever since there has been a queer grey dulness, but not a drop of rain until one shower this morning—and the garden all dusty and brown at the edges, cracks opening everywhere. P. came on Monday for the night and we heard about Italy together—Roosevelt's speech was great, I like his sobriety at big moments, and the cheering of the young people heartened one up. P. looked tired and distrait; but I think that everyone who knows France well must have felt torn with pity and anxiety for them this week; it is not that one feels

Paris must necessarily fall, it is how one knows they feel, imagining that it *may* fall. N., who came next day, has been quite heartrent, listening to the French broadcasts with tears of rage and misery in her eyes. . . .

P. has just rung up to say he's sending me some MONEY, as he thinks it's always a good thing to have beside one. I utterly agree, but can't think what he means and feel quite confused and foreboding. He asked if I had a bank here, was very hurried and said he'd ring tomorrow and rang off. . . .

SURREY
June 29, 1940

DARLING B.:

I can't tell you what an exhilaration it is to find that at this time one's friends are PERFECT, all in their different ways like steel. It's grand to know one always did like— as one thought one did—the best. I can't think of anything more awful than to find out now that someone you loved or relied on didn't really feel what all this was or know how to meet it—got side-tracked, like some of the French must have been, by fear of the people, by terror, by possessions. I don't mean the French *people*—I mean the scum that must suddenly have risen to the top, used Weygand and Pétain for its own ends, and sold France for—God knows what, their own security perhaps, or a safeguard against the Communism which, if it comes, they'll have done their best to bring about. The thing is, don't you think, we've got to have brains and we've got to have guts—it's just not the least use having one without the other, but the two are invincible. And I believe our Govt. now have both. . . .

SURREY
August 18, 1940

DARLING B.:

Well, John spent a week here putting up K.'s and our shelters and a lovely job he made of them. K.'s is in the barn and ours is partly in the ground by the back door and joined on to the wall of Mrs. B.'s bedroom. It has electric light, shelves, a long seat, a concrete floor, and holds 5 quite easily and 9 or 10 at a pinch. Roses trail over the sandbags and in fact it is a very dainty and Ideal-Homey affair and doesn't take up too much room to allow cars to turn round by the barn. Two days after it was up, air raids began in earnest and *did* K. and I pat ourselves on the back and put out our tongues (metaphorically) at the neighbours and tradesmen who had smiled at our sandbags, etc.

As I expect you've heard ad nauseam, there have been incessant raids this week—the most exciting was on Thursday when about 50 German bombers came right over us and dropped bombs (which hurt no one except a few chickens) in R—— and at B—— Court, about ½ a mile from here. It was about 7 and a most lovely evening. I'd just given Sue her bath when I heard a deep droning noise, no siren—so I went out to see, and Christopher, who simply haunts the house and is always using P.'s Zeiss glasses, rushed up to me and said in a voice quite trembly with delight, "Look, LOOK, there are hundreds of great German Junkers." So I wildly looked up through the glasses and my goodness, it was magnificent —there were the bombers coming up in a great V-shape out of the South-East (we heard after that they were only about 50, but they looked at least 500!) And suddenly 2 little Spitfires came diving down right under them and up the other side, firing like mad, a sort of high tat-tat-tat against the deep droning noise. They looked so tiny and heroic, rushing at those great bombers, it made you hold your breath—then the anti-aircraft guns began to fill the air with big black blobs of smoke and I suddenly realized what I was looking at, grabbed Sue, shouted to Christopher and Mrs. B. and was in the shelter in about 2 seconds. As we got in the noise was all up and down the scale—and one big BOO-OOP like somebody giving you a bang on the ear (the bombs at B—— Court, I suppose). Poor Sue burst into tears, trembling so that I had to hold her tighter and tighter, and wetting my dress right through, poor lamb. Christopher was splendid, he grabbed our new kitten, Darkie, who'd followed us into the shelter and held him up, all purring, and said, "Look, Sue, Darkie is purring, he *loves* air raids"—then Sue laughed and in a few minutes she was quite happy—and ever since she hasn't turned a hair, just bustles into the shelter and starts reading a book. And she isn't frightened at night or *anything*. And Janet and Sally are the same, so K. and I are very happy. Christopher of course just adores raids.

I must say I am glad I saw that sight and K. and I agreed it sort of satisfied something in our souls to hear those noises. I shall never forget the terrific droning as the bombers came up out of that lovely evening sky and K. felt her whole house shake as the bombs exploded—and to feel the children had seen and heard it too and come through quite happy.

Apparently as a squadron of our fighters came from the Dorking direction, the Germans swung round right over the pig farm next door and made off for the coast. They looked so invincible, and yet all they did was to kill a few hens and make Sue cry and wet her knickers, and then our fighters chased them out to sea. Oh, yes, they put our telephone and electricity out of action for a few hours by making some holes in the road and knocking down a few telephone poles. That was the day we brought down 160 German planes, and we haven't had anything as exciting since—though lots of alarms and A.A. fire (the anti-aircraft guns, by the way, have done superbly, 57 planes this week, and as soon as the fighters are in action they have to cease fire, even if it's an A.A. section)—and today we had to have lunch in the shelter—Dad and M. and Mrs. B., R., Sue and myself with P. and P—r standing outside and handing in claret and cider!

P—r is doing a special gunnery course in Kent for a

month and had 2 days' leave. M—l was here too, hobbling most painfully with a bullet wound through the ankle from a raid on some aerodrome where he was working.

PLUMS—B., I feel I shall never be quite at ease in face of plums again. I've bottled and jammed and jellied and pickled them till my feet are flat and my hands gnarled with stirring—and still the trees are *loaded* and plums come plopping down on to the lawn and are eaten by wasps and blackbirds. If I dealt with every plum on my 2 trees, I could feed a regiment for a year, and K. has NINE similarly loaded. We've also packed about 20 lbs. of beans in salt. I go over to K.'s for the News most evenings and we go bicycling, sometimes in to R—— to shop and sometimes just for rides, and it is lovely. The children pedal away in front and K. and I trundle along behind, gossiping and laffing.

Oh, B., a Frenchman is *singing* Verlaine's loveliest (in my opinion) poem, on the radio, "Le ciel est, par-dessus le toit, Si bleu, si calme"—singing very well as a matter of fact, but I remember reading it at Bowen's Court, 2 years ago, and what millions of years ago that seems.

P.S. Just got your letter offering to take Sue. Bless you, my dear, but I can't let her go—and now that air raids have begun we have our shelter and I feel sure I must keep her here.

DARLING B.:

I can imagine how sort of suspended and Mahomet-like you must feel in your exile—for it is exile, isn't it?—half in life, half out of it. I'm terribly glad if the broadcasts from here make a link with us for you. How awful it must have been when one knew nothing for weeks after it had happened, though of course better than knowing nothing ever of what is happening, or has happened, as in Germany. I wonder if you heard our young airman V. C. on the radio the other night? He was everything the idealized V. C. ought to be, modest, unassertive and, I heard, sweating and terrified of the microphone!

Did I tell you that K. B. C. is on leave and fixing up a telephone between K.'s and our shelter? Also that on Sunday a large party of us had our lunch in the shelter (the men pretending to keep watch outside but really enjoying themselves with their field glasses).

Having bottled, jammed and jellied plums, not to mention stewing plums and making them into tarts, I am now PICKLING plums—a beautiful deep red pickle.

Amidst universal disapprobation I am trying to buy some HENS. People keep on talking as if one kept hens for the sake of their society, saying, "Hens are so STUPID" or "Hens are so unattractive"—and urging pigs or goats. But a pig would be too much of a responsibility, alive or dead, and I just don't *want* anything a goat can give. The C.'s keep hens and a great big sullen-looking rabbit.

I went around all the cottages on the G—— road collecting National Saving stamps. The inhabitants were perfectly charming about air raids—as you know, though so near London, the cottages are remote and the cottagers real country people—and one and all believed that Hitler was aiming PERSONALLY at Mr. Swan's cows or Mr. Matthew Swan's hayrick, and were contemptuously delighted that he had had to send 50 bombers to do it. As I hitched my bicycle to each cottage gate, I would see somebody gathering PLUMS or smell PLUMS brewing in the kitchen. I shall always associate plums with bombs, if only because of sitting in our shelter in a perfect rage at knowing that my plum jam might boil over in the kitchen at any minute.

Did I tell you that K. and I went up to London last Wed. to buy shoes for Christopher and went to H.'s which was in a very dishevelled anti-customer, war-ridden condition—so unlike our dear P.J. or any other shop. I took myself to see "Night Train to Munich"—Naunton and Wayne, quite stomach-acheingly funny. It's a wildly improbable, exciting, nonsensical spy film. I wish you could have heard the audience laugh when a German official is made to say at the beginning, "At any moment now, our beloved Fuehrer's patience may be exhausted and we may be forced to attack Poland in self-defence." It wasn't a boastful loud kind of laughing, but a sort of happy gurgle, running all round, at a dear, thoroughly satisfactory, old joke which can never fail to please.

[99]

The vicar calls constantly and has left me the *Parish Magazine* with so many apologies and such obvious shame and horror that I have had to boost it to him for propriety's sake. P. has read it with devotion, of course, with the same relish that he reads our *Old School Magazine*. The advertisements gave him particular pleasure, specially one which had forced its way in with a kind of holy leer under the name of "Ye Olde Monke's Remedy—compiled under the shadow of peaceful monastery walls."

The blockade is going to be a bore, B., if your (I don't mean YOUR of course) business men go all saintly and humanity-loving about feeding starving Europe. It is unpleasant—it's HATEFUL—to starve people but it's just one of our weapons, same as U-boats are one of Hitler's—and Hoover certainly is in a rosy dream if he imagines he can get any food through the Nazis to the Belgians, the Dutch and the French. Of course this is just the sort of situation that Hitler, etc., loves—the cry goes up "Old Baby-Starving England" . . . and they may even get the French to believe it—but if it was my choice, I'd rather have Sue go short for a year than have her live under Hitler forever.

THE BUSINESS MAN'S WIFE

This batch of letters, addressed to the same individual, "B.," is from the wife of a manager of a London business. In this case, the eight-year-old child, Phoebe, is sent away with her day school to the country. Nearly all London private schools "evacuated" to the country on the outbreak. This meant, of course, that children had to be sent away from home much earlier than, in ordinary times, their parents would have thought wise. But no one of the middle class, even in the early days of the war, wanted to keep their children in the cities if they could find any other place to send them.

The husband, "S.," finding work slack at the office, goes to the country and joins the Home Guard, coming up to work in the day-time. The wife follows him wherever she can, but, when they return to London and the Blitzkrieg starts in earnest, she is at last persuaded to leave him and go to the country herself. An interesting change of tone can be seen in these letters; they start in a kind of exaltation in June, but end in November on a note of weary grim determination.

The Local Defence Volunteers (L.D.V.)—later called the Home Guard—was formed directly after the Low Countries were invaded. It accepted men over or under military age, and men who were rejected by the army either on grounds of health or because they were in a reserved occupation. They were to be used for defence at home. Within a few hours of the appeal for volunteers made by Anthony Eden soon after he took office as Secretary of War in Churchill's Government, the offices enrolling the men were crowded out with thousands of applicants. As will be seen in a later letter, even schoolboys home on holidays were eager to join. It is a hard job—and is done after a day's normal work. This means that workers on the land, or any other workers in country districts, spend most of the night—and indeed all the night if there is a raid warning—on guard beside roads, or in fields, or even sitting up in trees.

HERTS

June 10, 1940

DARLING B.:

I meant to write or wire you before you left but I didn't know where you were or when you sailed; but I thought of you and about how hard it must have been for you to go and what a difficult voyage it would be.

Just after you left S. got the chance to come down here and help B. with some war work. He is organizer of the Local Defence Volunteer Corps for his district (the parashooters) and the organization is really a terrific job, so S. is helping him with it. It suits him because he can get up to town 2 or 3 afternoons a week to keep the office going. I didn't want to be left alone in London so

came with him and we are living here as paying guests
with them. It is only 15 miles from London in a very
nice village and there is a quite charming garden. The 10
days we've been here have been blazing hot, so it's been
nice to be out of town and yet within a bus ride of it.
I brought I. with me, which was a good thing, because
the day before we arrived E.'s Austrian maid was interned, so I. stepped into the breach and is doing all
the housework. And now I find myself as busy as any of
them because I am doing all the typing and "office"
part of the organization, which is a full day's job, and
in between times E. and I brew innumerable cups of tea
for the men and run endless messages. There are nearly
200 volunteers from this village alone—pretty good—because it is no joke for these local ploughmen and post-
men and shopkeepers to do all-night duty in a trench
after a hard day's work. Most of the work is terribly
"hush-hush" and I already feel pregnant with military se-
crets! S. is really working fearfully hard at it and stands
guard at night too, sometimes. We haven't had a minute to sit and think about the news since we came here,
which perhaps is a good thing. One really begins to wish
they would begin to bomb England seriously because
then we'd feel the soldiers in France were being spared
just that number of bombs. After all, one soldier at this
particular moment *is* worth two civilians.

As you saw, travel to Ireland has been stopped, so I
shan't be able to go to Waterford with Phoebe in the

summer holidays, but I am not worrying because by then everything may be different.

I. is threatening to go off and be a nurse and of course I can't stop her for patriotic reasons if she really wants to do it but it will be a bitter blow. If she goes I shan't get another maid but do all the housework myself and make that my war job, anyway till the winter.

I don't know quite how long we will be here—it depends on how long the L.V.D. here takes to get organized and on all sorts of other factors. It isn't safer than London—in fact it's less safe—but it certainly is much pleasanter and the garden is a tremendous solace, I find.

Father * is well but the aliens restrictions do irk him rather—it seems awful that he shouldn't be able to stir from London without permission after living there 45 years, and it was a disappointment to him not to be able to get away for a holiday.

All the people we know in France in the B.E.F. have got home safe and unwounded. I think most of them are back again already, fighting.

Much love—you won't worry about us, I know, because you know S. and I are under a lucky star anyway, and this is where we *want* to be now.

HERTS
July 11, 1940

DARLING B.:

I was so glad to get your two letters—the one from the farm sent on from R. about a week ago, and then this

* An American—forty-five years resident in England.

[104]

morning the one you wrote on the boat. It sounds a terrible voyage; how funny meeting J. A. He wrote to S. at
the beginning of the war to say he was trying to find
some war work to do and couldn't. He is even more
American than S., having been born there. We find that
S. isn't really eligible for the L.D.V.'s, Father never having naturalized, and he certainly isn't eligible—on paper—
for the Army on that account, but I suppose they overlook these details in war-time.

Well, I don't know what news there is. In some ways,
there is a lot of news, in some ways none. We lead an
excessively simple and hard-working life—in fact, I sometimes feel pretty like a peasant! I haven't been to a
cinema or had a drink since we came here six weeks ago.
We are all working VERY HARD and in a queer sort of
way driving ourselves more and more, because it all
seems to rest in our hands now (as the posters say).
It isn't particularly that work is good for one's mental
state, because nobody I've met is jittery or nervy—less
so than at the beginning of the war, really—but just that
a tremendous conviction seems to have dawned on the
country that there is work for all of us and if we do it,
we'll win. It's really rather a cosy feeling in a way—no
loose ends, like considering "What will the French do?"
or "Shall we have to send an expeditionary force to
Siam?" or "Suppose Portugal capitulates?"—but just a
family having to set to and put a roof on their house
because there are no builders to be had, and it becomes

almost a game, instead of a bother having workmen trampling up and down the stairs.

E. has had to get a job, and rather an awful one, on the Assistance Board. She goes round houses of people in Barnet and neighbourhood finding out if they really are poor enough to have extra public assistance, and of course it is very tiring and depressing and she comes home every night worn out.

There is a good deal of typing and office work to do which I fit in with the housekeeping. The worst thing, I think, is the loss of sleep, because if there is any alarm of any kind—quite apart from the sirens—we (or rather B. and S.) get called out and the house stirs into terrific activity, with telephones ringing and cups of tea brewing; but perhaps it is better to be in the middle of things on these occasions rather than just passive. I typed "cups of tea brewing" but that touches on what has been for me, as you can imagine, a Major Tragedy of the war. Tea rationing started yesterday—2 ounces per person per week, which is about two-thirds of what I normally drank, and how I miss that one-third! But still, I haven't suffered the extreme anguish and agonies of smokers lately so I mustn't complain; but it is awful to have to think twice before having tea.

To go back to night-disturbances: S. has to mount guard one night in four, sitting in what seems to me a very uncomfortable position, up in the branches of a tree, in company with one of the local farmers or "blokes." But he says he is enjoying it because he says you get to know your fellow-man more intimately balancing with him on the limb of a tree throughout a damp night, than you would anywhere else—and I am sure he is right! They can't smoke, of course, nor do anything, literally, except chat; and they have to chat hard to keep awake. So by the end of the war he will be an expert on farming, in theory, at any rate, because they seem to talk about nothing else.

I can't even embark on our plans for Phoebe—because like all parents we discuss pros and cons and ifs and buts till our heads reel. The school considered evacuating to Canada and joining up with a school there, then they decided not to; then they thought they'd keep open in the holidays, then they found they couldn't. So it is left at the moment that when she breaks up on the 25th we bring her here (unless the Government issues a standstill order) which seems as safe as anywhere. They are raiding in the West almost as much as the East and we, being mid-way and right inland, north of London, seem to have been left fairly quiet. Four goats were killed three miles away (this was in the newspaper so can't be censorable) and we have of course often seen German planes, but that is a commonplace now. It is very expensive to take Phoebe to a hotel for eight weeks; and they seem to think they can have her here though where we shall all sleep I know not. I expect you have seen my letters to C. in which I said that the M. G.'s—among many other children we know who have gone to relations in U. S.—have gone to New York, with J. I under-

stand. Complete safety for one's child would be wonderful, but I am getting accustomed to the idea that we
can't have it for Phoebe at present. One advantage of
her coming here would be that we are near enough to
London for me to be able to take her up for a few hours
to have her teeth and flat feet attended to. Incidentally,
I had 4 teeth out last week.

I do think—if what we are told in the papers is true—
that it is quite wonderful the way people in America
have offered to take English children: people here are
very touched by it: and it's heartened them more than
anything to feel *practical* steps are proposed instead of
Notes and Expressions of Sympathy.

I really think you would notice the most enormous
difference here now, from when you left. The whole face
of the countryside has changed—no signposts, no names
left on hoardings or estate agents' boards or Tube stations—barbed wire everywhere, pill-boxes commoner than
public lavatories, *so many* soldiers wherever you look and
—very hard to bear—so many *English* refugees. The
Channel Islanders' plight is really pathetic, and now the
South and East Coasts are contributing their quota. One
really mustn't think about it because it is all only for a
time. We must get through this autumn and then it will
be better.

We are lending our house to a hard-up friend while
we are here—at least she is only going to use a bedroom
and the sitting-room and will—I hope—keep it clean for

me. It is only on a week-to-week basis so we can go back
any time. She will pay electric light and gas but no rent,
but as long as she takes care of it, it is a pity not to let
her have the use of it. I. is still toying with the idea
of being a nurse and if she goes, I am going to try and
manage without a maid because we *must* save money—
the future is so precarious.

I have piles of washing-up to do: am all alone in the
house today—I. was sent for suddenly to Canterbury
to see her mother who is ill and couldn't get back because there was a terrific air raid yesterday, the worst
we've had so far, and she was in the middle of it. So I
have had all the housework to do for two days—six people
to cook for (and I *still* can't cook!) and all having break-
fasts at different times and some wanting coffee and
some tea and all their eggs cooked in different ways—it
might be a canteen. Oh, if *only* people would lead or-
derly lives how much easier it would be!

Much, much love, dear B.—you really mustn't fret and
worry about us because as far as I can see people are
much more cheerful, even after all the appalling shocks
we've had and disillusions—than they were a few weeks
ago; and our defences are *so* good and will get better,
so really people aren't nervy and aren't counting on
America as they did, which is much better. There was
an awful point when people here seemed to expect the
sky over the Atlantic to be black with American bombers flying to our aid—now they know that if the children

can be taken and looked after that is all they can honestly count on; and it is much better to feel neat and tidy about things like that.

LONDON S.W. 1
September 19, 1940

DARLING B.:

I am back in London again. M. D. and I stayed on at Newquay naturally when raids began to be bad here— we went for a fortnight and remained for nearly 5 weeks —and *weren't* we tired of our old cotton frocks by then! I took Phoebe back to O—— Park yesterday and M. came with me, as these days it is better to have company. Fortunately we had a good journey there and comfortable in spite of being cross-country, with no raids. I left Phoebe there with feelings of relief because I feel she is as safe and happy there as can be. M. and I returned to town yesterday; her husband had been bombed out of his flat and had been sleeping here with S., but they both moved to the country yesterday as B. didn't want her to have even one night in London.

I don't know how to write of the last week, B. Last night was one of the worst air raids here and as it was my first I think it was particularly unpleasant, because the strange thing is you apparently *do* get used to them. But I was tired after 2 days' travelling, I suppose. I am sure I won't mind tonight so much. There was everything: incendiaries, delayed-action and high explosive bombs. I still can't grasp the fact that we are all living this fantastic life in a bombarded city. The censor allows me to tell you what is in the newspapers, so you know John Lewis is terribly damaged, and D. H. Evans and Bourne & Hollingsworth, Selfridge's and the Langham Hotel. Chelsea has suffered in various parts—Royal Hospital, Victoria Station. We are living now in a roped off part because of a near-by time bomb, but they think it is a dud.

We don't sleep in our bedrooms, of course, but in a very matey fashion on the stairs. I. and Ben the dog on a mattress outside our bedroom and S. and me on a mattress outside the sitting room. We sleep more or less dressed, and as these wretched time bombs necessitate people having to leave their houses suddenly till they're exploded, we have suitcases packed ready in the hall, and warm coats, always. The raids come every night the same time—8:30 to 6.

And life does go on. The office, after a 2 days' stoppage due to a time bomb, continues, though most of the staff take 3 hours to get to it. I picked my way over rubble and ruins this morning to buy kidneys at the Stores, and when you want to see friends, you ask them to lunch or tea, because everyone is bedded down in their shelters by 8 P.M. No theatres or cinemas to speak of: The "first afternoon" of a play by T. today. His fireplace was blown into his bedroom last night.

September 20th. Had to stop y'day because of a raid warning. We had a *much* better night last night—raid from 8.30 P.M. till 5.30, which means constant gun fire and sound of planes, but no bombs very near. Isn't it extraordinary that S. and I should now be leading the kind of life, approximately, that people led in Spain and Poland? Only of course we are luckier than they: better defences, better A.R.P. services (you can't *think* how quickly and well damage is repaired—it is quite wonderful), and better organization for getting food, etc., to us. If we can, we are going to try and get out of London for weekends, but of course country places are terribly full now with so many coast towns evacuated.

It must be too frightful for you and C. to read and hear of these London raids and be so far away. I keep wanting to cable every minute saying how safe and all right we are. The prospect of this kind of life is ahead of us, perhaps, but every night we get through is one nearer to winning the war. Americans are being awfully good sending relief and things—A. C.'s offer of a feeding unit was so touching I just *cried*—and it seems silly to say, like so many people before me, that aeroplanes and aeroplanes and more aeroplanes would comfort us more than anything. But I guess they're coming through too. The most nerve-racking thing of all, to me, is the steady throb, throb, of the German planes in the night with—apparently—nothing much to stop them. The anti-aircraft guns are like music.

How gloriously adaptable we shall be after the war! S. and I used to make an awful fuss at a hotel if we could only get a double-bedded room—and now we share a single mattress on the floor in the *greatest* luxury—and waiting 5 minutes for a bus was too awful—and now it takes hours to get anywhere. It must be good for one, obliquely.

I write on; really there is nothing to say that you wouldn't know and I can't describe our feelings because they're pretty obvious too. As long as this doesn't last *too* long—but I really think we have learnt the lesson of not looking ahead more than, say, a day and a night. I know you'll say, when you've read this letter, "They *must* leave London," but if you were here, you would see we can't. At least, S. can't, and naturally I want to be with him as long as I can. Also being a blood donor, they may want me. I'm the 3rd rarest kind of blood (very aristocratic!) so am not wanted very much. Only one I've given, since the first, but I have to let them know my address when I move. I'd like to get some kind of job—it is agony sitting around with nothing to do— of an unskilled kind, like canteen work, but it is difficult to get something that doesn't tie you—as I may have to rush to Phoebe any minute—or that isn't too dangerous, because I'm just not brave, and it would be useless to take on work which necessitated even the mildest kind of heroism. So I don't know.

Dear B., it is useless to say, "Don't worry," because of course you will, but keep on remembering that things are never so bad when you're *on the spot*. I learnt that at Newquay where all was peaceful and I knew things were happening in London—and in the American papers you hear about bombing and tragedy and destruction, but here I am discussing with I. what to have for lunch, and whether to have my winter coat shortened, and with S., in the evening, whether we shouldn't ring up and see if the So-and-Sos are still in London and couldn't they come for a drink (only beer now!) on Sunday morning. So keep all that in mind when you get over-anxious and worried.

I. is a marvel of calmness and cheerfulness—never seems to want sleep or get irritable. She is in her element because night raids offer endless opportunities of brewing tea, which is heaven to her; though we have only a meagre gas supply now, so kettles take ages. She has become very friendly with the local policeman who tells her a long tale of calamity every morning when she takes Ben out—we believe a quarter of it only—but she so loves telling it that we don't stop her. Her experience in Ramsgate raids had made her a kind of authority and she gives a running commentary from her landing at night down to our landing:

I.: Ooh, that'll be Marble Arch way.

ME: *Lovely* if they hit it—so hideous.

I.: Ooh, I'm sure they *must* have. That's a plane dive-bombing; hear it?

S.: Nonsense. Nothing of the kind.

I.: *Just* like the ones at Ramsgate. (*Pause.*) We *did* have fun in the shelters there. One day I ran out in such a hurry I had odd shoes on.

ME: Well, well. Come on, let's get to sleep.

1.: Wouldn't you like some tea first? We got a thermos here. No good keeping it hot for Hitler.

s.: Snores *(He's fast asleep—always is.)*

ME: Stop Benny scratching the blankets.

1.: Ooh, you won't mind about blankets after another week of this. Will she, Bennyboy? *(Period for nauseating dog-talk during which I doze and Hitler booms.)*

LONDON S.W. 1
October 19, 1940

DARLING B.:

I am now back in London again. I wonder if you saw the last letter to C. which I wrote from the country? I asked her to send it on to you because, among other things, it gave you the news of M. O. C.'s death—you might not hear otherwise. It was in an air raid—her part of London has been badly hit. There is nothing more one can say about it. I find it infinitely difficult to write letters to you all in America just now, and yet I must try because I know how you will want to hear.

I had a lovely 2 weeks in the Cotswolds—the bliss of sleeping in a bed and a nightdress was lovely. I walked and walked. My friend C. was there living with a friend of hers—the evacuated wife of a vicar in C—— with 3 children, who has very kindly offered to take me in and give me a bed any time—on a business basis of course—but for expenses only and not as an ordinary profit-making paying guest. As you probably have heard, the office

[115]

staff salaries have been cut and S. has had to give himself a cut of a third, so I could not luxuriate indefinitely
in a country inn. There is a possibility of my finding a
job there—there are several little factories doing war
work that have sprung up there recently—or I am willing
to be a shop assistant in the local town, and if I can land
one I will go back there and "dig in" for the winter. S.
really wants me to be out of London, I think. We have
Z. living here now—she moved from the O—— St. flat
when things got bad there and she is company for him
while I am away. She is *much* better and doing paid
work regularly for a Polish organization. Her book has
got marvellous reviews and is selling well.

I can't tell you how difficult it is to decide how, where
and with whom to live now. I am hopelessly torn between wanting to be here with S. and yet knowing that
I am a bit of a worry to him when I'm at home and in
many ways it is one's duty to get out of London if one
isn't doing essential national work. We discuss and argue
about it till we nearly go crazy because it is hard to be
apart too, under present circumstances. There is no possibility of normal home life in London now, and I really
don't see a great deal of S. when I *am* here as he is on
all-night duty every other night, from the time the evening siren goes till the morning All Clear, which is usually 12 hours, and the alternate night of course he is so
dead-beat he sleeps the same 12 hours. He has an extraordinary and enviable capacity for sleeping calmly even
when the bombs fall quite close and so, in spite of only

getting one night's sleep in 2 and working all day, he may get through the winter better than one fears. His stamina is quite amazing, as is his invincible calm and cheerfulness.

B., I don't really know how to write about the raids, how to convey a true impression without being overdramatic or sounding sensational or too depressing; or how much the censor passes of *fact*. Anyway, your own imagination must tell you what it is like to live in a heavily bombarded city and that is what we are doing—with the difference that we are English people being bombarded instead of Poles or Spaniards, with all that implies, and with the difference also that London was highly organized for just this contingency—so except in obvious circumstances, it isn't as messy as one would suppose. The heroes of this war will be the Civil Defence services—that's been written and said often enough—but the way they fight fires, clear up débris, rescue people, and do it night after night in every district of London, has to be seen to be believed.

We have 12 hours' hell every night, and in the morning London just gets up, shakes the dust out of its hair and smooths its clothes and by mid-day is kind of normal, but looking sleepy and with a bit more plaster and bandages on the sore places. You never—at least I've never—met anyone who did get used to the raids, to the zoom of the German planes, and the sickening sound of bombs. It's like giving birth to a baby—each time is bad —but you set out to have another one and you have it, and it's over. And every night we get through—and it takes some doing to get through some of them—is one tiny step nearer victory—sorry for the platitude but it just is so and it helps to know it.

Actually, compared to many districts, we have been terribly fortunate here. Bombs have fallen on the hotel at the end of the street and on the big square near, and 2 houses and a shop nearly opposite were burnt out 2 nights ago by an oil bomb. There is a *kind* of funny story attached to that. S. was helping an old man, stark naked, out of the burning house and found him a bit heavy to manage alone, so he called out to a man passing by "Take this man's legs, will you?" and as they walked carrying the old man, S. recognized a great friend of his at the other end of the expanse of the nude torso!

That is the way one meets one's friends in London nowadays. There is no social life at all, except perhaps for lunches, because everyone is indoors and bedded down wherever they are going to spend the night by the time the first German comes over in the evening and from then on London is just an organization coping with Air Raids—not a city at all. No theatres, a few cinemas. We still have the same bedding arrangements, each of us on a mattress on a landing—more or less dressed, and each with our emergency suitcase beside us. Time bombs necessitate one vacating one's house, suddenly and at any time, and staying out of it till the bomb explodes—so one must be prepared. The parts where time bombs are, are roped off—so getting about London is slow and difficult

—but transport too is marvellously well organized considering the difficulties. We've had no gas in our house
for a week and have to boil kettles laboriously on a tiny
methylated lamp—but we take our dinner every day to a
house three doors away which has a coal range and they
cook it for us and we carry it back. It isn't exactly piping
hot when it reaches the table!

The house is quite intact—not even a pane of glass
broken. I've taken elaborate precautions to protect my
nice glass and china from getting cracked with the explosions—but it is extraordinary how a building can almost literally reel and totter, and, like the inmates, be
unharmed and unscratched the next morning. But today,
as I was vacuuming the sitting room carpet, it suddenly
came over me how silly it was to be doing it, with a
house blown to smithereens near by—and yet one must
and does. One even renews one's kitchen utensils at
Woolworth's, and worries about moth in the curtains.
One must and does.

I see lots of vans—canteens and ambulances—in the
streets with "Gift of" some American organization on
them: and it is nice and comforting to see.

There you are, you see—this page sounds, in spite of
myself, as if I were being heroic and stiff-lipped and
everything. I'm not: I'm *terrified* most of the time. I
hate it and I wish it would stop, and I wish I could get
away from it and get everybody else away from it—and
yet I suppose I walk along the streets and ignore a new
bomb crater, and look mildly amused when the shop I

went to buy something at has disappeared, just like everyone else. We keep reading and hearing how admirably calm Londoners are—but what do people do if they're *not* calm? You just *have* to do your shopping and get your hair done—you can't for weeks on end scream and cry and panic—it's a physical impossibility—and the alternative is keeping calm. All very puzzling.

And now I hope I haven't given the impression, unwittingly, that London is in ruins. It is battered—there are districts where the damage is much worse than others, and a street of 30 houses, with 2 of the 30 completely destroyed, 3 more badly damaged, and 8 with windows out, is considered a very badly hit street—many many streets have no sign *whatever* of damage—some famous buildings are rather spectacularly ruined, others, of course not—the vast majority not. And the damage is repaired —in the case of craters in the road or house débris cleared —in a miraculous time. I believe I'm not supposed to name any building damaged unless it's been in the newspapers, but I think you'd love to know that so far as I know, no building that I know you would care about in a particular way, has been harmed, except one, historically interesting, which I feel you might mind. Otherwise, today, London is more or less as you knew it.

Later

Had to stop this to go down to the East End with P. Rather awful. But all the stories about the spirit of the

East Enders are true. They are angry, sad, but not in any way weakened. They want to go on and on fighting.

M. L. and Z. found an abandoned 3-weeks-old baby girl, in a sad state of neglect and starvation, in a telephone box a few days ago. M., good soul, took it home and they've got it going between them and arranged for it to go to a home in the country somewhere. Incidentally M. is doing a grand job of war. She and her daughter, on their own, not as part of an organization, take hot tea and cocoa to the shelters in the poorer parts of Chelsea every night and cheer the people up. She has become a kind of "lady with the lamp" in Chelsea, and unofficially does more to rehouse bombed out people and generally help them than all the officials put together. They all adore her because she understands them. She runs her estate agency all day—has her house full of refugees and homeless people, and does this shelter stuff at night. As far as I can see, she never sleeps at all.

This letter is all about affairs in England but that is presumably what you want. Do let me know about *yourself* when you write: I see a boat went down with a lot of American mail on its way to us, so I hope there wasn't a fat juicy letter from you to me in it. I get long and rather rambling letters from Aunt K., but am so pleased to hear from her, and a very sweet one from J.: and a letter from Uncle W. and Aunt E. offering to take Phoebe and/or me for the duration, which S. and I appreciated a lot. It all does help—to have this stream of good wishes and sympathy from America—if only an aeroplane could be included in every envelope!

Good-bye, dear B.—take care of yourself and write to me soon and don't worry about us. Life does go on, and one does get through things and as long as you keep your thoughts from going back into the nostalgic past—and so recent a past too—it's comparatively easy to keep going. Looking ahead always is better for one.

GLOUCESTERSHIRE
November 1, 1940

DARLING B.:

I think I wrote to you just before I left London. I saw S. was going to feel happier and sleep better if I were away, and so though it broke my heart to leave home again, I thought for his sake I must go. Also, if I were in the country, it would be somewhere for him to go for weekends regularly—and so get rest and sleep. So I came back here as Mrs. H. had said she would have me. Also, I wanted to get myself settled somewhere before the Govt. made evacuation *compulsory* for all unnecessary women, when I might have found myself in some awful place. Mrs. H. has been most kind to me. I have a pleasant room—huge and with a *gorgeous* view, but no carpet, no heat and no armchair. But really, after being in London, one is so thankful to have a roof and four walls, glass in the windows and a bed to sleep in that to complain is a Cardinal Sin, and mustn't be done.

She takes me much cheaper than I could live in an inn or, in fact, in lots of places and I share in the house-work and the discomforts in exchange. As soon as I got here, I set about looking for work. I registered at the Labour Exchange and within 4 days had landed a job—quite a good one in a way—at a Government Department here (can't be more specific, I suppose) and start on Monday! How queer it seems to be going back to work again—but I must do it. The hours are fiendish—9 to 6:30, every Saturday morning, and every other Sunday! The pay is goodish—£2.10.0—and just enough to enable me to keep myself here without calling on S. for money, which is what I wanted. The place is 6 miles from here—and I have to go by 2 busses—overcrowded country busses too—so I anticipate starting for work about 7:30 and get-ting home about 8, which won't be too much fun in mid-winter in the black-out. But it is *real* war-work, and quite valuable work too—and the hours are just the hours we must work in England, I suppose, to get the war won. It's pretty clever of me, I feel, to get a job at my age and state of rusty decrepitude! I woke up last night, having had a nightmare of being sacked the day I started! S. is going to try and get here for every other weekend—the Sunday I'm not working—so we shall get through the winter somehow, and we're lucky to be *able* to see each other.

If I succeed in keeping the job, I *can* have Phoebe here in the Xmas holidays. Plans for her go round and round in my head. Her flat feet have been pronounced so bad by the school doctor that she *must* go to the nearest big town to the school, where there is a good orthopaedic doctor to fix them, but now Miss H. and Miss W. write the road there is being machine-gunned by day and will I take the responsibility of her going? Her teeth badly need attending to—it is impossible to get her to a dentist.

Oh, B., I am sorry to appear to grumble like this. It makes me so *angry* that the world should be in this state where one can't be with one's husband or child in one's own home, or get the most elementary medical attention for her. She is just at an age when all these things should have been so carefully dealt with. But she writes happily and is well otherwise. I may consider taking her away from O. P. next term and send her somewhere more getatable: but next term?—anything may have happened.

I don't know what other news there is. Hilda M.'s death is in the paper this morning—not air raid, but after an operation.

THE UNMARRIED WOMAN

The last few in this batch are from an unmarried woman; a sophisticated and talented cosmopolitan. Having trained for First Aid work before the war, she was, to begin with, on duty at the post, during the monotonous months when nothing happened and A.R.P. service workers sat day after day at their depots, keyed up and yet very much bored. The letters start just after she has been transferred to important semi-official work in the country.

The exaltation felt by people of this kind is shown very clearly in these letters. For some years, many of them had felt acutely the horror and shame of living in a continent where Fascism had taken grip. They had also deprecated the part played by the British Government. Though they dreaded and hated war even more deeply, perhaps, than less imaginative types, they felt also that this particular war was the last chance that people of goodwill had to assert the principles by which they lived —it was, for them, a breaking out from the prison that Fascism was building around them.

The writer is the "N." mentioned in the second group of letters (June 13) and the "R." mentioned here is the writer of that second group.

WORCESTERSHIRE

August 6, 1940

MY DEAREST B.:

I am—as you know so well—dead tired sometimes, say today, after 6 days of night duty and no sleep except once, 6 hours, otherwise I just couldn't bear losing a moment's time, but it was lovely.

Well, I am in the midst of it now, in every sense, and I just do not care as long as I am in it. You would have laughed again, because, whereas in the hospital I was chosen for the mobile unit for my general je-m'en-fichism, here my work is unexpectedly that which I most love to do. It is most interesting work—I am happy in that, and our community is a scream and a delight. Not more funny than other communities, or any unit of people, but just more obviously so. And to live and work in the country is an added joy. The digs are good, the food plenty—though not on home lines—and everybody is full of new ideas, complete assurance and belief that at last we will build something worth while, even if ever so sketchy. And you know my predictions about France? Mother has got them in black and white from September 1938.

Of course I cannot imagine why *this* is called work. It is just enjoyment. I never before found anything which I would consider "work" something to sweat at. Sometimes I break my head over things here—but enjoy it so much that I do not think of it as "work." Maybe work is like that?

[126]

B., MY DEAR:

This war may last all our lives, and what then? Shall I never write to you because everything will be out of date by tomorrow? Well, aren't there other things to write about, which neither general human stupidity nor the Luftwaffe can smash or the censor take any exception to?

This island is more than ever a precious stone, B., you would love it. The people in London are so superb that one can never be the same after seeing them. And London looks more lovely than ever, as some people, mortally wounded, look lovely.

I was there last week, 3 days—and what is more—3 nights. People here thought I was mad to go, but I had to get it out of my system. Also I had to see that everybody who could, should get out of our house. It was a hell not to be missed. I wasn't afraid for a single second —but when I came back here to peace and quiet, I was shattered, and I shuddered at every noise.

Father had had a heart attack and mother had to take him to the country. She wouldn't have moved, of course, otherwise. She is as magnificent as the best of Cockneys. "I am not going to wait for victory by dressing for dinner in a hotel and doing nothing." However, the house became untenable and they found a cottage near M.'s.

During these nights in London our house became incredibly Russian. Our living room and kitchen and hall where everyone spent the night—Russians, very English refugees (my friends and unknown ones), Polish officers, Irish first aid nurses, aunts, German refugees picked up in the street—lamps on the floor, candles in the Saxe vases, a suitcase half open on the piano, with bits of old lace, junk, photographs; three cats, a kitten, the dog . . . and this infernal, really infernal noise, while all around things were coming to pieces, houses, streets, all were becoming dust.

With all this I am so happy here. Work becomes more and more interesting. The autumn is lovely, brown and silver. The country, the river, the swans at night—all like a late sonnet.

WORCESTERSHIRE
October 20, 1940

B., MY DEAR:

You cannot imagine what a joy a letter is from you nowadays. It is a link, it is a reminder, a hope. Yes, we will be different; we cannot be the same ever again after this. (As I write I hear a German plane overhead. The other day, one just like that, coming in the middle of a grey day, dropped bombs near us, just to get rid of them. It is the *hardness* of the noise that makes me furious with the boche.) We will have learnt to get rid of a lot of unnecessary things in relation to each other. Don't you worry. But *when?*

For obvious reasons I cannot tell you about my work. But I enjoy every bit of it. We are, nearly all of us, very much in the middle of death. We see it, hear it and feel it in our bones constantly. Some of us are more in the front line, and you know my attitude towards it. I have found that I am not afraid. The other day I went wildly mad about the late sonnets—do you remember the ones? —which are all bones and no flesh, quite spare, deadly desperate.

I am very happy in the middle of all this. But sometimes, my dear, "before a joy propos'd, behind, a dream" I have one wish—to hear you and W. just once more and have you say that everything is all right.

I am sad that I cannot see R. (it is impossible to get to her and London is more or less closed to us). She is marvellous in all this war life business—tough, desperate, radiant, brave.

Yes, Priestley is grand, we like him here too, and Churchill is great, and no one is greater than any Londoner today.

THE COMMUTING LINE

This second group in the "Day to Day Life" section is from women whose homes are, so to speak, on the commuting line. In some cases, their husbands work in London and go up to town every day. In others, their work is carried on in the small town or village in which they live.

Residents in this area, between fifteen and thirty miles from London, were officially considered to be "safe"; and the region was marked as a "receiving area" for evacuees from London. These women did not have the problem of having to leave their homes or send their children away. On the other hand, they had the difficult job of providing homes for the evacuated children and mothers, when they arrived, great crowds of them, bewildered and distressed, a day or two before and after the outbreak of war. Some of the difficulties and comedies are described both in this group of letters and in the group following.

People who live on the "Commuting Line" are very much like their opposite numbers in America. Each family lives in a separate house, not in a flat or apartment. Gardens play a large part in household life. There is perhaps rather less community feeling than in the "real" country, because there is less centralization; the local church does not play quite so large a part; there is no "large house" to be a centre for social activities. On the whole, people who live in these rural parts near London have not sprung from them: they have come to live there because they wanted to raise their children in fresh air, or because the cost of living is less than in town, or just because they do not like living in the city, although they earn their living there. But London remains the place which supplies clothes, entertainment and culture: and these are taken from London as and when required. In a way it might be said that the "Commuting Line" family is more of a self-contained unit in itself, and less part of a larger community, than either the London family or the family which lives in the "real" country.

Among the letters in this group is a series of five from a resident of a famous Garden City—a town which was deliberately laid out as a town-planning enterprise and became a model for several other attempts of this kind. It is not only architecturally planned, but socially planned. The land-owners, however small their holdings, have a stake in the town and are shareholders in it. Garden City dwellers are, consequently, civic-minded.

HERTS

January 22, 1940

DEAREST C.:

I feel ashamed not to have written to you before this: but I've been living in a perfect nightmare of busyness since the War began. We began by being *nine* in four bedrooms—of whom two were aged 76, two aged 12, one aged 9 months and one an expectant mother (who gave us, incidentally, a completely new insight into the meaning of the word "expectant"—there was nothing she *didn't* expect!). We finally persuaded the billeting authorities that even on *their* not very exacting standards we were over-crowded and they took the "expectant" away (praise God from whom all blessings flow! she was the worst of the lot, by a long chalk . . .)—then M. and our other small boy (a German refugee we had taken for the holidays) went back to their respective schools—and we then got a new evacuee, a secondary schoolboy of 17, who is a *dear* and fits in very well. Finally G.'s parents left us at the end of November and since then we have been practically normal, except that, not unnaturally, Anna left when the load was at its peak, and I am now the cook, having decided to have a nurse for the baby rather than another full-time maid. I am just in the throes of changing Nannies—the present one has been a nerve-racking experience. She is the world's worst chatterbox—about nothing at all—and having been in the Salvation Army, where she had to sell temperance leaflets in the bars of public houses, she has developed the hide of a rhinoceros, and greets all attempts to snub her with a forgiving and Christian smile! Luckily she has deprived me of the necessity of giving her a "character" by deciding to get married on Wednesday week. But I

suppose I shall have a few weeks' bother getting the new
one used to F. and vice versa.

I am longing to hear how you are all getting on. I've
just been reading Vera Brittain's *Thrice a Stranger*,
which gives a most alarming account of the expense of
living in the States! How are you managing? And how
are the children enjoying life? Have you met B. yet?
Oh dear, how nice it would be to meet for lunch at the
club and have a good gossip!

We had a very quiet Christmas and enjoyed it much.
Nannie went home for three days, so there were only
the four of us in the house. Our evacuee also went home
for a fortnight (strictly against orders, of course!—but
there *weren't* any air-raids, and it was a great comfort
both to his parents and to us!)

M. went to stay with friends at Twelfth Night [Janu-
ary 6th, the old Christmas Day], so I went off myself for
four days to J. C., who has been evacuated to W——
A—— with St. Paul's. (Poor old St. Paul's has been reduced from 450 girls to 180, and is completely ruined!)
I had great fun, as G. and his family are only three miles
from High W——, so I saw a lot of them. He is quite
a magnate in the shipping world now! and was very interesting about it all, tho' gloomy, as all the people who
ought to be in the know seem to be! They all say we're
in for three years at least. I wish I felt all noble and
crusaderish about it, but of course I don't. In fact I find
the only way to look at it is as a sort of frightful natural
disaster, like an earthquake, to be endured as best one

may. And it is extraordinary how *completely* happy one can be in one's private life in spite of it all. We are so amazingly blessed in being able to be all together in our own home, not scattered like so many families—and what does an evacuee or so matter in comparison with that?

F. is nearly fourteen months old now, and a *complete* love. M. is Top Boy at his prep. school and goes up for a scholarship at Ampleforth in March.

The following three letters are from one correspondent (the Garden City resident) to a neighbour who had gone to the U. S. A. The writer is a photographer—hence the reference to the "dark-room boy."

HERTS
May 15, 1940

DEAR MRS. H.:

Today we went up to the Glade and took a few little snaps of your garden. I shall be sending those shortly as they will probably not be ready to go into this letter. Please accept them as a little gift of sympathy for having to leave such a delightful spot. The garden is like a wall of green—the brightest cleanest green of May. The birds sing everywhere and the cuckoo is calling in the woods. Forget-me-nots look startling blue among the fresh green. Well, I just felt sorry for you. Possibly you are sorry for us now!

Today the police station is besieged with men and young boys joining up for home defence. Even my dark-room boy of 17 will have a gun and know how to use it. England has been slow to wake up. Maddeningly slow. I have talked myself hoarse and nearly choked with rage so often. But today they are well aware of the critical times and ready for any sacrifice. We have already rounded up one boy today who works on a stores' van. He had been a Czech, so his papers said. But yesterday on 3 occasions he had bragged to the staff that he was "after all German really." He has been sacked at once and taken to the police station to explain, if he can. We are all frenziedly Quisling hunting. I fear this place is a bit full of such folk. We have been so slow to think evil of anyone. The sad part is that if we do fail it is our very virtues which have brought us to this pass. We have grown soft with morality and our very goodness of outlook has blinded us to the brutal world of today.

Food rises in price and living is difficult. We get everything we want but at a price. Cauliflowers 20¢ and old carrots 10¢ at the very cheapest, they have been 30¢ a lb. Unthinkable? Meat is good generally and plentiful but usually only one sort at a time for some days. Lamb, lamb, lamb, until you are sick of it. Fish still good but too dear for more than once a week. Kippers gone utterly since Norway had its trouble.

The red trees are out in Bridge Road and everything looks lovely just now but no one can forget the seriousness of the war and its horror. I am training wardens in the putting out of incendiary bombs. I have a special apparatus and take twelve at a time and work on real

[135]

bombs issued to us at last for practice generally. My husband is still with the Fire Brigade and also on the Home Defence. We seldom see him.

Business generally is heartbreaking. We can't hold out for very long against this nothingness. And how to pay rising rates and this terrible income tax is a thing we just haven't been able to face out as yet.

HERTS

June 26, 1940

DEAR MRS. H.:

The Garden City is rapidly changing its character. Soldiers in every empty house and everywhere they stand on guard, changing guard every two hours, tramping feet and clanking muskets on the nice pavement stones— those big square ones so beautifully put in Parkway. Lorries rush to and fro and despatch-riders, all camouflaged in queer shapes.

Everywhere one is challenged on the roads and after dark we go warily and reply quickly if asked who we are!!

Food still excellent, but gradually certain commodities go from the shops. No Aertex singlets today to be found any more for my husband. He is heartbroken!! Certain soaps of well-known brand just go off the market and so, bit by bit, things change daily. The rot of war is setting in.

Life is much the same otherwise except that we all go

to bed very very early and hope to get rest that way. To be a warden is somewhat extra exacting but is well worth while. Both my girls are helping in the work. D. driving an ambulance and J. acting as a despatch-rider. Both being most sensible. The younger children are mostly to go, if it is possible. Homes are being eagerly sought abroad. They are wanted badly. Many have offered to have them and the whole High School is to be removed to another Continent *they hope*. Plus teachers. A good idea, that.

We take and take passport pictures. In one endless stream of hopefuls. The definite prospects of many are uncertain as the regulations do not allow children to go abroad unless they fit into some scheme or have a definite home to go to where the kind foster parents will guarantee their livelihood. It chokes me to see all this parting. Poor mothers.

HERTS
July 7, 1940

DEAR MRS. H.:

Thank you so very much for the papers which are most interesting to the whole family. It is nice of you to have thought of that.

Time marches on very rapidly here now. I wish I could tell you much which would interest you intensely. But the stern shadow of censorship has very rightly fallen upon us and the days of freedom are not yet once again! The spirit in England is *excellent*. We can never be beaten by our own people as has been the fate with so many other countries. And as we have no intention of letting the Germans beat us, we feel more and more sure of victory—however hard the meanwhile may be. Smiles everywhere and never a grumble. It is truly splendid. Sleepless nights are followed by happy meetings at the stores the next morning, and the events of war are mostly absolutely ignored. Not even mentioned. There is a fine race here and one which I would not care to attempt to defeat. Food is going downhill a bit now at last. High time. We have had marvellous food so far. But now there are no eggs at all today in the store and yesterday they cost 3d. each. But most of us have invested in hens and get our own. Our Henrietta laid her first egg yesterday and now we none of us feel we could possibly eat it! It is labelled "Henrietta" and stands in solitary state in the egg-rack. Waiting for more!

Bread is getting poor. Rolls horrid. But the shops are full of good things and if we can't have iced cakes, we can anyway have good cakes. Fruit plentiful but dear this year. Potatoes ruinous in price but excellent. We all eat less but that is to the good probably.

All day we take passport pictures still and mass-produce pictures of horrid and snappy type for identity cards. The cinema still flourishes. And D. still tours the country in repertory theatre. The young people all have so much to keep them busy that they seem to forget their troubles quickly. They are generally behaving excellently when there is trouble of a serious nature. It is the young children who suffer, as they don't understand. One small boy of 7 (whom you probably know) has almost gone out of his mind and they are doing all they can to get him quickly abroad. Just a matter of temperament as the sister went through the same experience and didn't turn a hair.

Everything is now in full leaf. Almost dusty. A really warm summer so far has given way to a few days of storms and low clouds but the wind is almost hot and this place still looks delightful with bright red roses in Parkway and well-kept grass (to my surprise and the extreme criticism of some folk who object to able-bodied people doing these things nowadays). Babies out everywhere in prams, half nude, with Mummies with short sleeves and gay frocks. It is like a baby-market still at 3:30 P.M. outside the stores—the inside too! Sometimes it is difficult to believe that we are in the midst of this grim struggle.

This letter is from the wife of a newspaper man, living closer in toward London.

HERTFORDSHIRE
July 19, 1940

MY DEAR C.:

It is good to know that in these days we shall be in your thoughts. I do hope that your people are with you, otherwise anxiety will always be preying upon you. Still, everybody here has a reasonable chance of safety, and no one is unduly perturbed. Perhaps because we know sooner or later we shall have to pass on. I do not mean that we are possessed by any kind of fatalism. The spirit of England is opposed to that, and a wonderful spirit it is expressed in so many ways; from the pride of a mother whose two-year-old trots at once to a shelter at the sound of a siren, to my good M. [the maid], who, reading that Hitler promised us a hot weekend, said, "Well, I hope that he has good weather." She always shows the utmost contempt for any Nazi threat, and if anyone gets a reward for undaunted courage in everyday things it is certainly she.

P. has been trying to write an article today, but two successive raids are not conducive to any continued thought; so he is still hammering it out. The wretches seem to come when we are about to sit down to dinner, or when it is in the oven and we have to turn the gas out. We only heard very distant gunfire today, and know nothing of the raid. J., who was evacuated and is back again, is generally out when the sirens go, she seems to take a peculiar pleasure in sheltering with different people, being shut up in cupboards under stairs, and in many strange places. We do not try to keep her in, the weather is so beautiful that we think tennis, swimming, etc., will help to build her up for the "black-out" winter.

We are following your American election keenly, and are hoping for all the speedy help that America can give. Your press urges that the help should come soon, the more you help the shorter the war, and more brave youngsters will live to continue the British breed. We are absorbed by the great heroism of our Air Force. In history there has never been such great courage. We feel proud to tears. Their heroism tears at our hearts. So many men want to join the Air Force. One of the newspaper clerks is going as a gunner and is busy studying until he is called up. The other clerk is going in the Navy; both men over thirty, who have never had time to play any games; just white-faced city clerks. P. says they are both such splendid workers. They are so eager to go, and are typical.

I do not think that any of us can visualize an invasion, though we know one may come. We are all confident that it will not succeed, but it will be eerie when we know that the feet of the enemy are polluting our shores. The only good thing that Hitler has done is to insist that German blood be German. It is good for all the races of the earth that their veins shall be clear of the Nazi taint. I no longer believe in any fundamental goodness in the German people. They are sentimental, sadistic slaves with the eventual cowardice of the bully. They are governed by the people they deserve, which is more than one can say of poor betrayed France. That separate peace was, and still is, unbelievable. It was a terrible thing to face and the consequences have made our hazards harder. Still Churchill and the Gov't. have faced up marvellously. The hour has brought the man for us. And we are grateful.

Do write again when you have time. You will get our

news in your paper. I do wish your press would not be so insistent for instant news. An air raid on London should not be a Roman Holiday. Goebbels can invent a bulletin packed with lies, but we are concerned with the defence of our people and the routing of the enemy, and until our men have chased them across the sea, and returned, we cannot check or issue any story. We have to wait for news and no one minds. And one had to wait longer in the Crimean War! I doubt if B. would have mentioned G. if our Air Force had not brought down every raider; not one returned to report.

Rationing is a great stimulus to the English house-wife. We shall really have a varied and strange diet. There is no privation at all, and as the minds of our people govern their bodies, they can get used to anything. We all find that we do not want more. But liking the nice food of the world I would like to drop in on you and have a Maryland chicken with corn and strawberry shortcake—or is it too late for strawberries? We'll do it after the war.

I do hope that all the family are well, and that they have not been worried by the heat wave. It has been one of the most perfect English summers, the roses have surpassed themselves.

Two letters from a writer living near Epping Forest.
H.E. is High Explosive bomb. A Molotoff Bread-Basket is a kind of portmanteau bomb which when it explodes releases incendiaries.

ESSEX
July 16, 1940

DEAR H.:

You would be tickled if you were to walk down Wood-berry Lane now. I have a notice in my window which reads "SERVICE" and this means that in the event of an air raid and if a person is injured, the A.R.P. men are able to bring him or her here and I am to provide hot drinks, blankets, bandages, or ice until the ambulance comes to collect the victim. Nearly everybody has a no-tice of some kind in their window. There is a "W" which means that a pail of water is available. Others have "P" which mean that they have a stirrup pump. (Incidentally we have a sixth share in a pump, but if anyone thinks we are dashing out in an air raid to fool about with one of those infernal contraptions, they must think again.) Just inside our front door we have a shovel with long handle and a pail of earth. With these things we hope to deal effectively with fire bombs, but as we shall be in our dugout (we hope) I am afraid the house will be burnt up before we discover it. Outside the front and back door there are pails of water, so you can see how seriously we are taking to our obligations. I have also cleared the loft of inflammable materials, and trunks, etc., are in the hall. The house looks an awful mess with all these preparations, but I just don't care a hoot, and I haven't the heart to finish the spring cleaning.

ESSEX

October 8, 1940

MY DEAREST H. AND R.:

I am afraid I am going to talk a lot about air-raids, but will put it off as long as possible and answer your welcome letter first.

With regard to sending you news and your comment that the Government seems to be releasing more information, I am afraid that we are not very satisfied here. When we grab the *Telegraph* in the mornings it is just a survey of the news bulletins of the night before and so disappointing. I notice that they try and push our air-raids to the background and give precedence to our raids on Germany. I am probably quite wrong but I don't feel so happy about these raids as is the tone of the press, because if they are able to clear up the mess as quickly as we do after raids, it will take a very long time for air-raids to be effective on either side. I can only hope that our aim is better than theirs. I am pleased that our letters have not been censored, since you warned me, but we are being very careful.

Now I can't keep away from air-raids any longer. We have had them incessantly for the last five weeks. Of course the night raids are just awful and start about 7-30 in the evening and go until 7 in the morning. The gun barrage is terrific but we don't hear so much of it as people who live in the S.E. For the first three weeks I don't think that I slept more than an hour a night, and we all felt pretty tired, but not in the least shaken.

For some reason the barrage was not used at first and we could hear those awful machines droning ever nearer and bombs crashing closer and closer until we all felt that we could scream at the inactivity of somebody or other. There was much more damage done in the first fortnight than has been achieved since.

Oh! the sight of London burning was horrible. Great flares that seemed to envelop the whole of London. It looked to me like a child's nightmare of the end of the world. It was a ghastly sight, and I'll never forget it. When you see something that you love and have lived with all your life wantonly destroyed and know that thousands of people are being killed who ask for nothing more than the right to live and work, when a little home that has taken years to get together is just smashed before your eyes, you will imagine the feeling of all these poor homeless people who are struggling to get away from the danger area. We've had three thousand refugees in C—— and their plight was pathetic but not once have I heard anyone hint of giving in. Their one idea is to fight like hell and get even with them. They are truly wonderful. When you see a little shop and a row of houses smashed beyond recognition and one or two tattered Union Jacks flying above the wreckage you realize more and more that we just can't be beaten. If we entered this war lethargically, we're bumped out of it now. I talk to the tradesmen and ask their opinion and they all say, "My God, it's hell, but we're not giving in, let us get at them." They're just fighting mad about it.

Night after night D. has picked up refugees in the car and just dumped them into the forest. They have no idea where they want to go—just get away from the dock area. There are many large retreats and halls near here where these people go for a night or two and then they are sent away to the country or other safer districts.

For nearly three weeks we had no gas, and I struggled with cooking on an ordinary electric heater, turned on its back, and when D. was home, a Primus stove. The thing terrified me, and I couldn't make the beast work anyway. Fortunately, we are all right now, but the bath is kept filled with water! We've had H.E. in N—— C——, quite near, and a Molotoff Bread-Basket in Woodbury Way. This is a packet of fire bombs which burst in the air, and fall just anywhere. Heaven knows why they bother to drop a thing like that here.

We heard the thing burst and the patter, patter of the bombs as they fell in the road and all around, and here is an amusing thing. D. wears a tin hat. He is very proud of it, and during a raid wears it all the time. This night we were dozing in the shelter, when we heard this thing drop. With one accord we leaped out, and what a sight—fires, flares, smoke; it looked as if the whole town was ablaze. D. dashed into the hall where we keep a bucket of earth and a long shovel and tore across the road and helped to put one out which was burning somebody's fence, then went on to another further down the road. Then U. saw two blazing in the forest at the bottom of the garden and tore down with a garden spade. I, in the meantime, running and tripping behind them, falling over the end of my dressing gown which caught in my legs and threw me every now and then. The wardens were on the spot spraying their special pumps and doing their stuff, and would you believe it, in half an hour there wasn't a thing to be seen. Two hundred bombs and in thirty minutes—finished. The joke of the thing is this: when it was all over, and we went back to the house for tea, D. put his hand to his head and said, "My God, I forgot my hat!"

Another amusing thing occurred the other night. It was pitch black and D. and I groped our way to the shelter when, suddenly, I heard something whistling down. I couldn't run as I had an armful of eiderdown and coats, so I did the only thing I could do, threw myself on the ground. Unfortunately D. didn't know I was so quick witted and didn't expect such quick action. I went down and he fell full length over me, kicking my head and cutting his hand, not seriously. I was quite convinced it was a bomb, but it turned out to be shrapnel.

D.'s brother's house in W—— was blown up. And Grampa H.'s house was damaged when one fell on the next house to his. It couldn't have been a very big bomb or the two would have collapsed like a pack of cards. He was talking on the telephone at the time and as he is rather deaf had no idea that the planes were overhead, and that bombs were dropping. So far, he has refused to leave his house but I hear that he is going to Work-sop with his housekeeper.

You know, H., I can't understand why they bother to drop bombs in some places. They obviously throw them overboard to get rid of them. Both W.'s house and Grampa's are nowhere near military objectives. Grampa's faces the forest and W.'s is purely residential. W. and J. have been wonderful. They lost everything and the house next door came down too, but they are cheerful and courageous, and not a bit depressed. J. said, "Well, I always said the house was jerry-built. Well, now Jerry has knocked it down."

I can assure you this courage is a very real thing. It is amazing how people carry on. The mess is cleared up, the hole filled in and hey presto, who said there was a bomb?

Last week I made a special effort to go to town, to get some winter clothes. The autumn is creeping on, and I hadn't anything to wear warm enough to take me through the winter. During the day we had five air-raids, but nobody bothered. Everybody went on selling and buying, and going about their business. I was scared when I heard the first warning, and wanted to bolt for the shelter, as it was my first experience of a raid in London, (I haven't been able to get away from the house for weeks). When I realized that everything went on as usual I felt more reassured. But I was quite glad to get home again. Poor John Lewis's—it is a wreck, just a charred skeleton, and also Bourne and Hollingsworth's.

The latter are still open, and as I walked through the smashed ground floor all the wreckage that had not been removed was covered with Union Jacks, some of them were dirty and tattered, but nevertheless, Union Jacks. Everyone was so cheerful that I wanted to weep. From one tiny attic window in J. Lewis's, they were lowering wooden boxes of soiled pink corsets and brassieres. Waiting below were hefty salvage men and assistants collecting them and putting them on J. Lewis's van which was waiting for them. What on earth is the use of bombing shops of that description? They are no loss to the country, have no military value and no strategic importance. They are still carrying on, everyone helping and cheerful—so what? Lewis's are opening a small department in the next block, and everybody will buy from them as soon as they can to help them on their feet again.

I seem to have said far too much about air-raids already, but there is so much to say. After all we are completely obsessed with them. We can't see our friends, or do anything very much these days. There is no time. As soon as we have finished tea, I rush up stairs and change for the night, siren suit, bandeau, socks and thick shoes; U. also. I prepare a light supper, tea, or snack. D. gets home at seven and before we are finished the siren is wailing and we are listening to the guns when we dive down under. Sometimes I manage to wash up, but usually I don't, and U. and D. creep back to the house during one of the lulls and finish the washing up and lay the breakfast table. Everyone helps and D.

is a perfect dear, rushes around and does all kinds of jobs. Shopping is a problem as most of them close during a raid and when the "all clear" sounds everybody rushes for their goods. The shops are so jammed full that it is impossible to be served. There is plenty of food but not so much variety. I think the Gov't. is tackling the job most thoroughly, with the least amount of delay. How they manage to keep supplies going to an ever-changing population is beyond me, and whatever criticism is thrown at them, they do get things as quickly as possible and are always thinking of new ways to help and relieve distress and, above all, we have plenty of food. Thanks to somebody's foresight we haven't felt the raids at all where food is concerned. Even the morning papers usually arrive for breakfast. The one thing that has gone to pieces is the telephone, but when one thinks of the enormous strain on their limited capacity and the amount of additional telephoning that must have taken place in the last few weeks, we try not to grumble about it.

This is a disgraceful letter but there have been three air-raids during its concoction, and dinner prepared and eaten, and now another raid, but daylight ones don't bother us very much unless we hear them overhead. They are never so terrifying by day, and often there is a good air fight to watch.

Three letters from an English "Nannie" to her ex-employer, whose children she had looked after for 10 years until the very day when they sailed with their mother for the U. S. A.

SUSSEX
August 30, 1940

DEAR MRS. M. G.:

Thank you so much for your lovely long letter.

This part of the country comes under the fighter command where our planes go up to chase the Nazi. They have been at it all day, but we are quite used to it. I have made three attempts to get my washing in, but each time there have been fights going on. We ought to take shelter but it is so exciting that we just have to watch unless they are very near.

The two younger boys have been out for a picnic lunch today, and they came home full of excitement because they had been able to watch the air battles from their rock caves.

I went to London yesterday. They had had a four hour raid the previous night, and everybody was very sleepy but otherwise very happy. The Nazi have tried for the Air Port where N. lives, they got quite near. N. says there have been several bombs dropped near Mrs. A.'s house but she is still there to tell the tale.

The air battle is still going on at this moment, but one can't spend one's whole day in the basement, and they are too busy to drop bombs around here.

I was noticing air raid shelters in people's gardens on the way to London. Some have rockeries with gnomes

[151]

and rabbits on top. One had marrows growing, and another had a nice crop of red tomatoes.

R.'s friends say they are getting quite attached to their shelter. They have seats all around with nice spring car cushions so they can continue their sleep in safety.

Thank goodness the children aren't frightened, it seems awful for them to get so excited but it is better than having them terrified. There were a lot of flares dropped the other night and it was like a fireworks display. We spend all our evenings watching the searchlights following the planes round the skies. It is quite impossible not to get excited when they shine right on a plane.

The All Clear is just sounding so our planes have managed to chase them home, but they will be back again later. It is 6.45 P.M. now and the raid has been on for almost four hours now. The one we had this morning lasted longer, and was so near that we could see the swastika on one plane when it crashed.

Don't think that we are blasé or that we don't know the danger. But one does get so used to hearing the planes and the bombs.

I have not been in a public shelter yet, but G., aged ten, was out on his bicycle and had to spend just over an hour in a shelter. I asked him what everybody was talking about and he said, "Oh! one woman thought her coffee would boil over, and another said her dinner would be ruined."

I will write again before very long. I was hoping I

should have had to go into a public shelter in London to see for myself how people in town are taking it.

SUSSEX
September 1, 1940

DEAR MRS. M. G.:

I forgot to thank you for the pictures of the children. R. seems to have grown and I am glad they are having such a happy time in and on the water.

The Germans were busy last night, and it really doesn't give one's curls a chance. I had just washed my hair and set it into a beautiful page boy bob and I had to take the curlers out before it was dry because I had to go down to the basement and did not know who else might be there.

The children are very nice here but the place is so isolated that there are new maids coming all the time and even for twice the money I could not face the winter here. I was in the boxroom the other day and saw the prams. They are white with their initials on the side. I should feel horribly conspicuous pushing a white pram.

Old Jerry must have had enough round here yesterday because there hasn't been a sound all day. If anyone had told me this time last year that I could sit and eat my dinner whilst an air battle was going on over one's head I would not have believed it possible, but the truth is, I do it.

Last night there were lovely coloured flares dropped. They may have been our own. I don't know.

I must stop now because I haven't answered the children's letters.

MIDDX.

October 9, 1940

DEAR MRS. M. G.:

I arrived here Monday. The Manor is being closed and Mrs. J. is going to an Hotel to live. When I got here I went to Mrs. G. as I knew that No. 2 was closed. After I had knocked at the door, the woman in the next house came out and the following conservation took place:

MRS. P.: Mrs. G. has gone away.

MYSELF: Oh. I will go to Mrs. W. then.

MRS. P.: She has gone to Newcastle to attend her father's funeral.

MYSELF: I am so sorry, I will go to Mrs. B.

MRS. P.: Mrs. B. isn't there, her house has been bombed.

MYSELF: How awful! Well, I shall go on to Southall and see Mrs. A.

MRS. P.: I am afraid she won't be at home either as her road had to be evacuated because they had a delayed action bomb there.

At this point I gave up, put my luggage in N.'s coalshed and went to Hounslow to get some lunch. However I did go to Mrs. A. later and found her at home. She was very pleased to see me, and we had a long gossip during which she said, "Well we used to put the cat out at night, now we put ourselves out and the cat in." They sleep in their shelter since the two houses opposite had a direct hit.

Mrs. A.'s daughter came round while I was there with the loveliest baby of six months. I admired the baby and his pram. Mrs. A. said, "He's got such a lovely cot, all frills and bows, but he has to sleep on a shelf in his Granny's shelter."

I wish I could draw a picture of their shelter. Ma, Pa, and Betty sleep on a mattress on the floor. Mrs. A. has put a shelf all around, her daughter sleeps on one side, her husband on the other, and the baby at the head. Mrs. A. offered to make room for me on the floor if I was afraid to stay alone. All the people sleep in their shelters. I looked at N.'s and found beetles, spiders, and worms. I decided I would as soon risk being bombed as to be frightened to death so I went up to my room.

N. is here now, and she sleeps in her bed too; I can sleep through the noise of the sirens and guns, but awaken when the people come out of the shelters and start talking about 6 A.M.

N. has got a young couple living here. The husband is a soldier and stationed at Heston, but his wife is here because their house at Poplar was hit. They are very nice and had a large thriving business (eel pies, etc.) before Jerry got them.

[155]

The following is a reply to an offer from friends in the U. S. A. to give hospitality to the children of the writer.

HERTS
October 25, 1940

MY DEAR C.:

I know it's frightfully remiss of me not to have written to you after your most *awfully* kind offer to have both the children. Please forgive me—life has been hectic. We did both appreciate your offer and know what a huge undertaking it would be and awful responsibility, having someone else's kids to look after. Thank you both very, very much. We just couldn't let them go. The danger on the sea was too great and we do feel living in the country like this, we all have a good chance—anyway a sporting chance, especially as M. is at school in a similar spot.

So far we have had great luck and long may it last. We've had 14 bombs dropped round the house—some, 250 and 300 yards away. But there is one marvellous comfort, when a bomb drops it does give you time to lie down when you hear its zizzing through the air.

I've had a good deal to do lately and often been on duty for 3, sometimes five nights a week. We've had bombs dropped on the vestry of our church (which was great luck as it didn't matter and just missed the East end and it's a lovely old church). Still it has done about £1000 worth of damage. Then one went through the kitchen of the pub in the village, and sent the publican's wife flying under the kitchen table while the whole kitchen broke all round and she escaped with only shock and a cut. We had our back door jammed and a few windows (no broken glass), some plaster off the house and stables. One bomb has yet to go off.

D—s is quite unafraid and is only slightly worried because she can't distinguish between guns and bombs. "I'm not frightened, Mummie, but I would like to know if they are guns or bombs." It has been rather hectic as we have my father, aunt, my sister and D.'s secretary all here and, for a good long time, no maids. Now we have a real peach of a cook.

Bother, there goes Jerry overhead so I suppose the sirens will go in a minute and I must then be off to the depot.

Our R.A.F. boys are simply wonderful and of course we shall win through however badly we get knocked about first. D. has almost all the windows broken at the office, but isn't he lucky that the office is left—one can't help feeling terribly grateful in spite of his having no water or gas up there. Anyhow we can get paraffin and I sent him up with two oil stoves yesterday. It's wonderful, he only goes up three days a week now and works at home the rest of the week. It's pretty awful the days he goes up when London gets bombed, but still we can thoroughly enjoy the four days he stays behind in spite of everything. It's a great blessing too that there is still work coming in to the office although D. has no lecturing to do now.

I had a frightfully thrilling day in town lately. The first time I'd been to town since Christmas. I caught the 7.15 A.M. train and started shopping and got in quite a lot before the siren went off at 11 for an hour. Then again at lunch time I had to go down to the air raid shelter, where I bumped up against D.'s father and old General G., who had just lost the ceiling in his house and was feeling rather peeved with Hitler. Then I dashed up, finished my shopping, caught the train and had another air raid warning by Hackney. Near Ponder's End, we saw a *marvellous* dog fight, you should just see our Spitfires. Then the big German bomber burst into flames on one side and came down straight for our train. She *just* lifted and crashed the other side of our train into a sewage farm. Of course we couldn't help it, we yelled and cheered our Spitfires. It was awfully thrilling.

There goes the siren, I must go on duty and finish later. Later. That was a long wait but they've all gone now. *Oct. 30th.* D—s and M. are growing up fast and are awfully good friends. I do hope you will all come back when the war is over. We are feeling awfully bucked up, how well our R.A.F. is doing and we've had some lovely peaceful nights lately.

It's not really fun being out in air raids but with so many fields round one feels mighty glad when they drop there as it means so many less for the towns.

I am afraid this is all about the war, but we are all

feeling so cheered up and even if they drop lots more bombs on London well they can't possibly win, and our people in town are just *wonderful*. Well I simply must stop.

Thank you, C. and S., ever so much for your kind and generous offer and should we ever feel it best, well, we shall gladly accept.

COUNTRY DWELLERS

In most country villages the war came dramatically and literally to the doorstep in the shape of evacuated mothers and children on the actual morning of September 3rd, as will be seen in the third letter of this group. But it did not need the evacuees to bring the war close to villagers. In 1914-1918 remote villages in England were sometimes hardly conscious of war, but the radio, the black-out, the flow of leaflets from the Government on A.R.P., had made everyone fully aware of this war before it had even started.

Still, village life, though somewhat surprised and dislocated by having to accommodate a large number of strangers, went on in the usual way; even a few cricket matches were played in the summer, though these had to stop when the Home Guard was formed and all the members of the village teams, from 17-year-old boys on holiday to the oldest inhabitants, volunteered for the duty of keeping their fields safe from parachutists and invading troops. The Women's Institutes—a nation-wide organization of village women's clubs—continued to hold their meetings. Church was rather better attended than before, although Evensong was shifted to the middle of the afternoon (in winter) because it was not possible to black-out church windows.

The village in England clings to its individuality; even when a town or city encroaches on it, so that it is practically swallowed up in suburbia, it still feels its distinctness as long as any of those residents are living who remembered it in the old days. And so long as it is not actually swallowed up, it manages to preserve its rural nature however often trains may go to town and however short a time they may take to get there. In Surrey, for instance, there are villages twenty miles from London, some of whose inhabitants have never been to London—nor show much anxiety to go. The village is the oldest unit of society in England; to many, it represents England more completely than does London or the industrial north.

The centre is the church—usually a Gothic foundation with unfortunate 19th-century "restorations." It is surrounded by a graveyard in which, more often than not, three-hundred-year-old tombstones, finely carved and lettered, will be found beside those of yesterday. There may be a green near the church, with possibly a duck-pond. There will probably be a "public-house," with its inn-sign hanging from the front of it and a wooden bench not far off. Round about will be a few small shops —no more than cottages with a slightly larger front window in which is shown a dusty advertisement card of somebody's branded goods, a couple of jars of "sweets" and some vegetables. Inside you may buy a limited number of foods, including buns, vegetables and sweets, and

probably note-paper, pins, and odd selections of clothing, like stockings, overalls and hair nets.

Cottages run along the street, not in quite a straight
line; one or two of them with plastered walls and
thatched roofs; one or two of red brick, straight-fronted—
a century newer than their plaster neighbours; one or
two, or far more, the work of modern local contractors
and not very decorative. Somewhere further off, set back
in its own grounds, there is probably a large house, where
the biggest local landowner lives. And stringing along
between this and the next village, also set in their own
grounds, will be the houses of the better-off—other land-
owners, well-to-do farmers, or city people who have
bought or rented a place in the country. Some of these
houses are modern; some are Edwardian—red brick with
perhaps a touch of neo-Tudor; others are fine, gracious,
18th-century manors; others, again, date from still further back.

There is a great deal to do in the country. There is
the garden which provides work during most of the year.
There is walking to and from the village for small pur-
chases. There is going into the market town for stores
and meat and clothes. There are the various meetings—
Women's Institutes, Church Meetings, Bazaars. There
are social activities—garden parties, tennis parties, cricket
matches, and so on. There is, in certain districts, all the
to-do connected with hunting and shooting. And by the
way, neither of these two activities is entirely confined
to the "upper classes," as some people suppose. Still less

is this true of village cricket-matches, which are thoroughly democratic institutions.

Among the "Country Dwellers'" letters are included some from people who live in country towns. These small towns are simply extensions of the village, but their social and commercial orbit is the county—or a section of the county—rather than the cottages and houses in the immediate neighbourhood. Here are sizeable shops, chain stores and cinemas. But the local feeling is just as strong, and the interest in your neighbour's doings almost as marked, as in the village. The names of the country town's streets are very old names: its growth can be traced, almost house by house, for at least three hundred years. It thinks a lot of itself. Its main street is probably wide, flanked by Georgian or Regency shops and houses; its side streets are narrow and may twist about, or suddenly become lanes or land you into open country.

There is a large-ish public-house—it may call itself an inn—with a courtyard behind in which coaches used to draw up before the days of railroads. The butcher has "home-killed meat," and over his doorway may hang a basket of ferns. But country towns pride themselves on modernity. The bright frontages of Woolworth's and other chain stores inject a wholly up-to-date note.

The first letter is from a lady of seventy in a very small village, with a population of less than two hundred.

February 4, 1940

DEAR MRS. M.:

Your delightfully long and welcome letter deserves a speedier answer than this. At my rate of typing (I am slowly practising the correct fingering and without looking) and with many interruptions it may well be several days before it gets posted.

I feel I ought to have acknowledged your cheque for the Church Council which I now do most gratefully. It was all the more welcome as we have lost several subscribers lately. Fortunately our expenses have not been heavy, so we ended with a balance of £40.3.5 last year after paying our full quota of £28 to the S. London Church Fund and distributing £41.18s. in "charities." I hear that the attendance at church services does not improve and that the Vicar is prone to make the same mistake that his predecessors did—of scolding those that do go for the absence of those that don't. He has a houseful of evacuated children—four with B. and as two of them are biggish boys who attend L—— Central School you can imagine that they make some noise! Mrs. B. finds it pretty trying together with all the extra work involved and I am rather afraid she may break down unless things are made easier for her in some way. Mrs. H. and I have tried to make the Vicar understand the situation, but one can't interfere beyond a certain point.

These children at the Vicarage and one or two others

at the Bungalows and one at Mrs. B.'s represent all that
this village has at present in the way of evacuees. We
prepared for about 30 and twice got to the point of waiting with cars at the School to receive and distribute
them, but each time they were absorbed in L—— instead. This was because the teachers wanted to keep
them together as much as possible. They are all from
one neighbourhood and entirely fill the L—— Central
School so that a somewhat elaborate shift arrangement
has been devised by which both the local and the evacuated schools work under the same roof though not at
the same time. The local W.V.S. [Women's Voluntary
Services] has been doing excellent work in running the
canteen for the mid-day meal for both schools. This in-
volves feeding 300 children in two shifts between 12
and 1. No light task! And it is heavier just now owing
to the almost complete lack of vegetables caused by the
hard and continuous frost which has lasted up to last
week. Most people have suffered from it in one way or
another. Frozen and burst pipes galore, cracked cylinders
which have put countless cars out of action for many
weeks and in some cases months, etc.

My neighbours at H—— are very kind in giving us
lifts, but Mr. H. who requires a car more frequently has
to go about in an old hired rattler for which he pays
2½ guineas a week. With a petrol ration of 5 gallons
a month one misses the car less than one would otherwise.

I bought a bicycle to help me out and hope to make considerable use of it when we get better weather.

I hoped that our Austrian refugee maid would like to use it and feel less restricted in her movements thereby, but she has proved quite incapable of learning to ride! She does not become less of a problem as time goes on and we have finally decided she must go as she will never be responsible enough for us to feel we can leave her alone in the house when we want to go away. It will be better for her, too, to be somewhere where she gets more variety and sees more people. But the difficulties in the way of getting her shifted are gigantic. The fact that the Tribunal put her (along with all but 2 of those that came before them) into the "B" category—permission to move within a 5 mile radius only —means writing to the Home Office to get her case reviewed, etc. and if this fails I am told it will take 6-7 weeks to get her into a new job *after* one has been found! In the meantime I have given her 2 months' notice, and you will be amused to hear we are going to have X. back. "The evils that we know, etc." She has misgivings lest she has become too much of a rolling stone to settle down again, but is quite ready to have a good try at it. I believe she said she has been in 8 different jobs since she left us.

Mr. R. is Head A.R.P. Warden. Can you picture him taking round and fitting gas masks? He had a nice time with some of the babies, I believe!

I too find it difficult to say anything about the war.

It is hard to get away from it when it confronts one at every turn, whether on the wireless, in the newspapers or all the little changes in one's daily life. One welcomes little distractions, and from time to time makes deliberate effort to turn one's thoughts in other directions, if only to return to it with some freshness.

Certain parts of the north of Scotland, from which this woman farmer's letter was written, were "protected areas" into which no unauthorized person—and no aliens whatever—could enter. Stores or weapons were kept there, or there were training grounds for certain troops or airmen.

Farmers were kept busy with government orders and regulations. They were told to plough up more land for food growing; grants were given them for drainage; committees were formed to give them advice or to demonstrate. Government inspectors came round to see that everything possible was being done by every farmer to help supply the country. There was a good deal of exasperation and quite a number of mistakes, both from above and below; but nevertheless a great deal of hitherto wasted ground was put under cultivation and a great deal of grim devoted work was done.

The writer is a woman of over fifty, who had been for many years an active political worker in London, and who had also travelled widely, before retiring to a remote part of Scotland to look after her aged mother, and to run a large sheep farm.

[167]

November 2, 1939

MY DEAR C.:

I wonder how you are getting on.

We don't see much here—a few bombs spread about, an occasional mine blowing itself up against the rocks, various convoys trapesing up and down the Sound and of course the ever present and ever changing instructions issued to food producers by the Govt. At the outbreak we were exhorted to cope with the submarine menace by increasing our flocks and ploughing up our impoverished little fields. Having done this at great expense we are left holding the baby, as the Navy and Merchant Service cope quite nicely with submarines unaided. Also we are in a "protected" area, though from what protected no one has been able to discover. But we can't go to [the nearest town] without a Nat. Registration Certificate, Certificate of Residence, etc. An ordinary passport is no help at all but rather a hindrance as if you hopefully produce it its number is merely endorsed on one of your other documents and henceforth you have to have it also. Practically no one is allowed to enter this area—holiday makers being particularly barred—so we can't get summer tenants and the little people who depend largely on visitors for their income are badly hit. However we all regard it as our share of the war and only hope there is adequate reason for the prohibition.

Mater—now 92—and L. are as usual. H. still intact and with her windowless house sheltering five little shopkeepers whose little businesses are no more. However no one is really upset, merely thinking what a prize ass Hitler must be to think we would give way.

Send me your news sometime and tell me about the family. Meantime my love and good wishes for Christmas.

These two letters are not strictly speaking from a "country dweller" but from a London schoolteacher who was evacuated from London with her school. The evacuated teachers had a very difficult job. They were the link between the strangers from London and the village or townspeople on whom the children were billeted. They had to clear up the varied misunderstandings and resentments that of course often arose. They had to calm down the worried hosts who found some of their evacuees never took baths or that they had skin troubles. They had to explain to puzzled children that it was better and more natural to eat fresh vegetables than canned ones, which is what they were used to. They had to keep matters calm and clear between their own staffs and the staffs of the village or town school whose premises they were to use; arrange timetables so that a whole day's work could be fitted into the half-day they were allowed in the schoolhouse. They had to see that in this half-day the children under their control did not run wild. The worst thing of all for some of these London teachers— who have a legitimate pride in their school and school equipment—was having to fall back on all sorts of make-

shifts in order to carry on the curriculum without the equipment they were used to.

Sometimes, the school was split—sent half to one village and half to another. Sometimes it was enlarged, because two of the same family would be evacuated together, even though they had not attended the same school before.

The teachers had no time for holidays or days off; they were isolated from their families and removed from their homes. They have done a very heroic piece of work.

The L.C.C. referred to is the London County Council, under whose direction are the London schools. A "neutral" area was one from which children were not evacuated, and to which no evacuees were sent.

KENT

January 11, 1940

DEAREST C.:

We have been through great upheavals, but I am fortunate enough to have kept my job. I had had four days of my summer holiday after helping with Summer School, when I had to return to London and help evacuate the children. About 200 of them are down here, billeted in the town and round about, and we are sharing the T—— High School building and an extra overflow house.

I was billeted at C—— when I first came down, but it was eight miles away. Now I am sharing a small flat with another of the Staff. O. was appointed liaison officer to all the Youth Organizations in the Midlands, soon after war broke out, and she had to go live in Birmingham. So we packed up and moved from the flat last week, and I brought most of my furniture down here.

J. had an evacuee mother and baby for some months before Christmas, but in her last letter she told me they had left. That part of the evacuation was certainly a failure.

Some of the London schools are already returning en bloc but the L.C.C. refuses to let us consider it, and we are certainly in an unhealthy district with Woolwich so close. How I have envied people like L. in a nice dull neutral area.

I have been chief billeting officer for our party, which has meant lots of work, not all of it pleasant. I still can't enjoy ringing up or visiting perfect strangers, and trying to persuade them to take unwanted children. But it is interesting to know where all of them are, and to know their hostesses and to see how some of them flourish away from home. On the whole we have been very fortunate, but it is wretched never to be able to forget what is behind it all, and how far we seem to have wandered from sanity and safety.

My flat-companion is a most able musician and has her piano here, and it is pleasant to be reminded now and then by music of some things that can never be touched or harmed.

May 26, 1940

DEAREST C.:

Well, we are still here though there is talk daily of our being declared a "danger Area." But things happen so quickly, that one never knows from day to day how much history is going to be made before bedtime. We are exploring possibilities of another migration, but so far I don't think that Miss L. has found any place for us to go. It would be an awful upheaval, so much furniture etc. was transported from London. There are about 200 children down with us now. So we are all hoping that we don't have to shift. I had to find two billets all of a sudden for children whose hostesses decamped to safer spots. It is very awkward when hostesses begin to flit.

My brother E. is just finishing his training in the R.A.S.C. but I haven't heard yet where he is going to be sent. He joined up some months ago, and was given his Commission on the strength of his membership of the O.T.C. John is 32, so will be called up shortly. P. is making efforts to be released from her contract to come back to do war nursing. I think that the Govt. will allow this in certain cases. Mother refuses to leave Norfolk though M. and her husband have invited her to go and live with them further inland.

I have just been enjoying Eliot's book *The Idea of a Christian Society* though I must say it required a great deal of hard thought. I do think that he is so wise, when he maintains that we must get clear what we want to put in the place of what we are trying to destroy. I have recommended all my Sixth form to read it. They are perusing with great interest occasional numbers that I put up in their form room of the Christian News Letter, which Dr. Oldham inaugurated last year. We are supposed to be studying Comparative Religion this year, but constantly I find myself having to stop and discuss all sorts of other questions such as "Why need we have Religion if we have a good Government?" or "How can we make sure that we don't destroy ourselves with our own civilization, by letting the spiritual side of ourselves drag behind?" It is very interesting and very hard work, and it is very difficult sometimes not to be pessimistic without being insincere.

We are having the most heavenly Spring. I don't think that I've heard so many cuckoos in the last ten years. One of the results of migrating from London! I sometimes go out to C—— at the week-end to visit the family whom I was billeted with when I first came down. The bus drive is a perfect delight.

My Lambeth diploma is proceeding so slowly I sometimes think it will never come off. I am so busy, with no free periods from teaching, and dealing with billeting problems in any free time I may have.

I am completely cut off from everybody down here, and don't seem to have had news of old friends for many a long day, and now letters are so costly.

The writer of the following letters makes several references to the evacuation of government offices. Many large offices and factories evacuated from London to big empty country houses at the outbreak, and their employees were billeted in the district. Quite a number returned before the winter was over—the difficulties of carrying on business under these conditions seemed greater than the risk of disruption by bombs; besides, the employees could not often take their wives and children with them and the splitting up of families caused much distress.

"Queen Anne's Bounty" deals with the distribution of that historic grant to clergymen.

The writer, who is nearing sixty, was entitled on grounds of health to a medical certificate which relieved her from the obligation to take evacuated children; though she feels able to cope with expectant mothers, who were also given free evacuation opportunities by the Government. They were given a pink card for their railway pass and some amusement was caused by the B.B.C. when it gave out the official instructions for evacuation, because it delicately referred to these women always as "pink card mothers."

On Sundays, the husbands and fathers of evacuees used to appear and in most cases the hosts were kind-hearted enough to give them lunch or dinner so that the family could be together as uninterruptedly as possible on the one day they could meet.

During the year her large country house was taken over by the Government as a billet for troops, and she

*moved to a flat in a neighbouring country town, where
she is an active W.V.S. worker. The second letter tells
that story:*

SURREY

January 24, 1940

MY DEAR C.:

In a way we suffer from the same thing as you—isola-
tion. Everyone is so concentrated on their own job that
one seems to see nobody and hear no gossip. The broth-
ers say the same thing. In their case it is partly because
they all have to be at work at 9 and altho' offices close
early, the upper ranges don't finish any earlier than of
old. So far as I know the India Office is still at its
normal abode, but ½ the Ecclesiastical Commission is
down near here—½ Queen Anne's Bounty is at Cuddles-
don and so forth. Brother G. came down here to act as
billeting officer and at the beginning was coldly received,
until it was realized that by having respectable clerks the
farmers escaped verminous children, when the attitude
quite changed! The main difficulty was baths, I understand.

Evacuation is still the unfailing subject on which we
are all eloquent. Of course the big schools have a mighty
grievance but if public offices had been obliged to get
out of London they could not have used the country
houses to which schools have gone because there are not
billets enough handy.

In my case it all worked out rather wonderfully. I got

[175]

rather slowly over the tonsil op: and was able in consequence to get a medical certificate—but didn't use it when I found I could have expectant mothers instead. What did rather discourage me was that not only was "our Sid" (naturally) called up as a territorial, but quite unexpectedly H. was called up as a permanent fireman and I'd nobody even to stoke or feed the chickens.

Picture me on Sunday Sept. 3rd sitting by my wireless in the drawing-room window listening to Chamberlain, when Mrs. S. C. and 2 cars full arrived with suitcases, and paper bags complete. Luckily for me they were nice women, except one, 7 of them (5 expectant) and 3 small children. The latter were all "only" and combative but quite attractive and when one could keep them amused peace reigned. It was very interesting to see how soon they ceased to want toys and took to making mudpies in the garden with any old thing that turned up. I think the most successful game of all was a hunt in gasmasks for a stink-horn.* We shared rooms—meals—expenses, 2 of them cooked and we all did our own rooms.

It was interesting to find we lived for less than 7/— a week each—good carving by one of them being the reason I think. We had the most comic lunch parties—the fathers and my friends. One day the new Vicar came and one of the "expectants" said afterwards, "We did wish we'd known he was coming, we'd have put some powder on!"

* An extremely strong-smelling kind of fungus.

February 13th. Here I take up my story again, having with great joy seen the birth of the desired little daughter on Feb. 6. Perhaps you will be able to come back before the 10 years are out—how I hope so. But one feels that the future is going to be very queer. I do think you would say if you were here that there's one encouragement in the way it is all being taken. I'm forgetting tho' that you aren't my contemporary and may not remember the way we looked at things in 1914. But oh, dear, how ghastly it is—Finland and thousands of dead Russians. However, glooming doesn't help, does it?

SUSSEX
October 24, 1940

MY DEAR C.:

First I must tell you why my address is as above. We had at long last got a good let for our former home which for obvious reasons I will not name. I was preparing to go at a week's notice and the idea was I should store my things and look about. Suddenly the house was requisitioned in mid-June and we lost our let and I had to go at 48 hours' notice and just then when things were at their worst no firm would—could—store and it was impossible to get anyone even to move you. With great luck I found and took a flat over the shoe shop in this country town and a lorry went to and fro with H. and R. and myself aboard and somehow we got it all in. The flat is too expensive really and unnecessarily big, but it has been so good to have a chance of further sorting, whittling down, and I can't tell you how I have in all these awful times enjoyed arranging my own home. It is what I always wanted, to live in big rooms—my sitting room is vast and will be cold I'm afraid very soon—and the pick of the family things look so nice.

Of course now the whole place is stiff with soldiers everywhere and we think nothing at all of tanks and other exciting craft which would have sent us all running to look of old. Here in this town there are road barriers all ready to go up if invasion still comes and you get accustomed to locking your car every time you get out of it and dismantling the what-you-call-it arm. Not that I have anything to do with cars now—I declined G.'s when I came here as garage was almost impossible and petrol had to be fetched from some way off. So at 58 with amusement I bought a bicycle and I go about on it with a rucksack. I and two other old ladies do mending for a nursery school three miles away and I go to and fro with that.

Getting about takes much longer than usual. Brother R.—you will remember where he lives up on the hill—frequently takes 3 or even 4 hours getting to his work and back. You get decanted at B—— or some place like that and then do your best. I stayed up with R. and V. for a fortnight—very lively times up there of course and our R. used to get home, change into his fireman's kit (he commands the local A.F.S.), dine hastily and "on the siren" repair to his station there to spend the night till the all clear in the morning. So many people sleep in their clothes nowadays and still survive. I don't know how they do it. While I was with them the first attacks on London came and never shall I forget the awful sight of the fires and the feeling that nothing could be done. One quite understands the relief with which we heard the barrage start. The refugee people here complain no end because they don't hear guns and do hear isolated planes. Isn't it funny?

Brother-in-law H. came safe home from Dunkirk. He was at G.H.Q. and for a fortnight they had the most terrible time. He went through 5 years nearly in France before without any bitter feeling about the Germans. But this time it is very different since he saw the awful things done to refugees on the roads and all that.

The whole Dunkirk story is a proud one, isn't it? I met a young gunner here who was at St. Valery, which was almost worse. He said, "When we got to Portsmouth we all lay in bed for 3 days and the W.V.S. women brought us our meals there and all the barbers in Portsmouth were had in to shave us, our beards were half down our necks."

One very wonderful thing I think is the way we are fed. There is absolutely no shortage of anything and no extortionate prices. Eggs are expensive, but no wonder, and even then not what they were in 1917.

Some people find it difficult to have only 4 oz. a week of bacon, but we share round and things equalize up.

My job here is to be woman on duty in the air raid shelter down below my flat. At first it filled up at once when the siren (which is generally pronounced sireen to my amusement) went but now it is a very dull job because only 2 or 3 old people or schoolchildren go and sometimes no one and yet one must not leave it to chance. One day it was only 2 tiny Jewish children from the East End who had brought in a vast packet of razor blades which they said they would "put back on the dump when they had done with it." I gathered they were picking out what they thought might be of use to Dad. We have here dumps in all sorts of odd places in which we throw tins and mowing machines and all sorts of quaint objects which are metal. It is rather a cute dodge I think—small dumps everywhere so that no one can have far to go with his tin.

F. is a cook at the Middlesex Hospital and has a fairly hectic time sometimes—"we cook where we safely can, all over the place—" she says.

(Pause while I dash out to see what all these low planes are doing—nobody knows whether they are hedge hopping or what but no machine guns seem on so I suppose it is all right.)

Time bombs are a bit of a nuisance to us at times because people have to vacate their houses till they have gone up.

Owing to the shelter job and 3 half days a week at the W.V.S., I scarcely ever get beyond the streets and Mrs. S.'s gifts of flowers and potatoes and one day a cooked chicken are most welcome and touching.

26th October

P.S. This was written at the W.V.S. office. Now I'm at home sitting by my fire at 8 P.M. thinking I really must go and boil my egg. It is a most unpleasantly bomby night—that swooping plane we all get everywhere and it gets near and shuts off its engine and then bump, bump and the windows shake and you wonder where the next will be.

I see on re-reading my letter that I did not tell you how our one-time home has had R.A.S.C. men, R.A.M.C. and now another corps there. The footpath and green are a regular park of same.

H. is still there, single-handed, and he has a fairly hectic time being a fireman as well.

In both your letters you speak about the things we have to put up with—for my part it seems to me astounding that we really have so little to complain of. And it is most wonderful and cheering that the "young entry" we all felt so doubtful about have turned out so magnificently. It is difficult to see how things can develop for good, but we all feel quite sure they will.

So with much meaning I say "au revoir."

The next four cheerful and equable letters are from a twenty-eight-year-old girl to her sister in America. The writer is running her own farm near the same country town from which the previous correspondent was writing. There is something very typical of England in their practical gaiety and unsententiousness.

[181]

*The question of London refugees, or evacuees, as most
people called them, again arose in September when the
London bombings began. But even at this time, the number who took advantage of the Government's offer to
remove them from danger was very much smaller than
had been hoped for.*

*A letter from "Aunt H." appears among the section of
letters from* The Older Generation.

SUSSEX
September 22, 1940

DEAREST H.:

I am afraid it's a fortnight since I last wrote (incidentally I think I misdated my last letter by a day) but B.
was here till yesterday from the previous Saturday and
what with one thing and another I didn't get down to
it. It's been as you will know an awful week for London,
but nothing very outstanding has happened here. Miss
P. was at their produce market the Friday before last
when they got some bombs very near. Her nephew had
just left her there and gone on up the hill when one whistled by him. He threw himself down at once and was un-
hurt, but a woman quite near him was hurt and subse-
quently died (though I don't think she would have if
she'd been a reasonably strong person). There's a couple
of houses with half their roofs gone but that's about all.

I actually had a party last Sunday evening. We played
hilarious games—drawing snap, etc., and had great fun,
and nobody left till midnight in spite of the fact that

R. and M. had been up all the previous night with the Home Guard, so it was quite a successful party. B. went to Tennis at the S.'s with me last Sunday, we went up to Aunt D. G. for tea and games one evening and she went into [the country town] to the cinema with J. another afternoon, but for the rest insisted on making herself useful, so I taught her to plough and we took turns at that while the other played around or did odd jobs near by. She really did quite well—no serious blots on the field. We're busy on the G. L. field at present. I went out again yesterday evening after B. had left until F. came and stopped me because there were such a dickens of a lot of planes going over; and I have been there again this afternoon till it got too wet, when I came in and washed my hair.

L. came down last night to ask us to take homeless refugees from London. He was in again today talking to Mum. They weren't expected till "some time next week" but 100 have already turned up. They've got to doss down in the village hall tonight but we're to try and be ready to take some tomorrow. The flat being empty we're going to put them there. I did tell you didn't I that the B.'s had left, to try poultry farming on their own again. We haven't collected anybody in their place yet.

I heard from P. not long ago. She said it was too much of a good thing with the children having to get them up every night so she's taken them to Wiltshire for a month or so.

Aunt L. persists in staying at the flat in London though

they've had an awful lot of damage round there. I think it's chiefly because the refugee cook can't leave her restricted area and she doesn't want to leave her alone. She's trying to get her papers changed now though, so that they can both come down to Aunt H. for a bit. Aunt L. seems amazingly cheerful about it all—says she only wishes they'd come over in bigger formation so that we could get a really good crack at them!

SUSSEX
October 6, 1940

DEAREST H.:

We were wondering what had happened to you or what we'd done to offend, when at last—the day before yesterday—we got a letter from you.

I think Mummy wrote in her last letter to you that I'd heard your tenant, Mrs. H., is giving up the flat. She's just got through to me on the telephone (I'd tried to get through to her 3 or 4 times, but it was always "restricted service" to London on account of raids).

Would you like me to pack away all except the furniture and just leave it, or get someone to come in and do it out a little bit once a fortnight or once a month or something? You might answer this however belatedly for then if I've done the first, I can always make arrangements to do the second instead. I think Mum told you too that there'd been a bomb in the courtyard behind, but only some broken windows and no damage to yours.

Mrs. H. is leaving because her husband is being moved to the country. I thought she sounded nice. She said one thing was worrying her—2 wine glasses and one ordinary were broken and she can't match them anywhere. Am I right in thinking they were Woolworth? I didn't say so to her. I haven't yet looked in your drawer of papers re the flat, but fear there probably won't be any evidence.

If I don't have to spend the entire day in a shelter or stranded somewhere half-way up I shall quite enjoy going and seeing what it's like up there. Aunt L. has been staying with Aunt D. G. for a week, but is going back to London on Tuesday. She says, "It's no good my pretending I mind being up there, because I don't." In fact nothing will persuade her to stay away from the flat, and I don't think it's entirely because of the cook. She admits that one doesn't get an awful lot of sleep. If it weren't for the loss of life and injury, I can't imagine anything better than having the slums blown up for us free of cost and it seems to be there that most of the damage has been.

Did Mummy write you about our refugee family? We've put them in the granary flat and all seems to be going well and happily.

We've had some pretty noisy times but nothing very much nearer. There's supposed to have been a timed one quite near about a week ago. I heard a funny swishy noise and the people in the cottages heard the same and then a thud which they were certain was something arriving in the meadow just behind. Both cottages evacuated till morning and though the Home Guard and the Army have searched and searched nothing's been found anywhere. Most peculiar but it happened near by before. The sounds must travel extraordinary distances. A. was with me for a few days spending half her hard-earned holiday here, and like B. set-to and really seemed to enjoy working the tractor. Of course we don't get through more than one would (especially as I always had to change gear for her) but it's more fun and doesn't keep me away from it. I got a shock yesterday as C. fell and caught his ribs on the side of the lorry and they thought he'd bust some, but the doctor says only wrenched a muscle and once strapped up will be O.K. I had awful visions of trying to do it all including the field to be ploughed for the first time. By the way I was awfully bucked when the War Agriculture Committee man came and did his inspection. He reports them as "badly," "mediumly" or "well farmed" and we got the last which is apparently rare. He was a nice kindly old man, so perhaps it was just to encourage.

Do write a really argumentative letter and tell me what everyone thinks about the relative importance of helping to the east or being watchful to the west. That scrap-metal business is grand. American Commentaries over here continue to report that Willkie is so far miles behind Roosevelt.

We went to tea at the H.'s yesterday, a party of 15 and rather fun. R. is now organizer of a great number of canteens and spends a lot of time in the dock areas.

She says there is an awful lot of delay and red tape to shift, up at that end, but I must say from the receiving end it seems wonderfully well done. Our lot came without any warning and within a day of their arrival billets were arranged for all of them, and their papers through about the next day so that he could draw his unemployment money and we could get our billeting money. Did I tell you the nice remark someone made the other day about the great advantage it would be if only we would try using red elastic! *

Your leaves were lovely though I think they must have faded a bit, and pleased Mummy very much. I think we've had it lovelier than usual here this year. Those Japanese cherry trees opposite have been absolutely flaming scarlet.

I went up to call on Aunt D. G., Aunt L. and Miss S. this evening (really to get Aunt L.'s advice re the procedure with inventories, etc.) and though in a frightfully disreputable state got roped in to help entertain three young officers who'd been teaing there. One of them being H. I nearly fell down backwards; he's 6′4″ if not 6′6″. He'd more or less hitch-hiked all the way from W—— to come to tea and it took him so long he had to turn round and start back in ½ or ¾ hour! We're very busy now with ploughing and sowing and the thrasher's in at last too.

* This is, of course, a pun on red tape.

SUSSEX

October 17, 1940

DEAREST H.:

To start with about your flat. I went up to London as planned. It looks generally a little less fresh than it did (paint, etc.) but nothing I think that one could complain of. The chief tragedies are the loose covers, but there again I don't think you could complain—it's just honest old age, worn to holes in places and faded. Your tenant had replaced all breakages except one small plate which they said would take 6 months or so to get, and five bits of glass. I've covered the books and groups of smaller furniture, etc., with dust sheets and the porter's promised to go in and open the windows. The curtains rather worry me. I've taken them down and shaken them before folding them up but they are rather grimy and I don't know if it'd hurt them to be left like that. I do hope it's O.K. I am afraid the chances of another let are probably infinitesimal.

My expedition to London—the first since things got at all hot—was all rather interesting. My train got in punctually and I proceeded to set about my shopping. I went first to Oxford Street and no sooner arrived than the alarm sounded, but as nothing happened at all I proceeded. Lewis's, as I expect you've heard, is practically non-existent, with tragic looking half-burnt remnants still on the pavements—rolls of silk, etc. Several other shops are in rather similar plight but the general effect is not at all of widespread destruction—just here and there.

I then went to Harrod's, looking quite normal, and got a cardigan set for R. Then I went to 43 for lunch with J. and J. It was all quite fun and too matter-of-fact for words. Then I rushed to your flat and started the work, had a cup of tea with the tenant about 6, and went to H—— Street. It was all shut up and I was just giving up in despair when a man went up the steps next door and I asked him if he knew anything. There was a "W" on the door so I asked him if he was a warden. He said no, he was "just nobody—had been in the Finnish army, then the army in France and now was just nothing." A weird individual, but he told me to wait and re-emerged from next door with a scrap of paper with the right address on it. My strange informant said he was glad to help and I needn't tell anyone who'd told me! All v. odd and mysterious.

I then went on to Victoria and found the last train home didn't go for ¾ an hour so I went to see Aunt L. as I knew she had a parcel she'd like me to take down to Aunt H. She gave me some remains from lunch as quickly as possible, but just about 20 minutes before my train was due to start, the fun and games started (about 7.20). Aeroplanes clearly audible overhead and terrific anti-aircraft fire all round. Aunt L. told me I mustn't go out but I was still considering making a bolt for it when we were told by a warden that no one was being allowed near the station, so I had to give up. Aunt L. put me up a camp bed in the passage outside the door, saying that it was much pleasanter as well as safer not to be near an outside wall. It really was pretty terrific. Aunt L. said it was the worst they'd had, apparently they've been concentrating on that neighbourhood. (I'm afraid it was probably even worse the next night.) You could hear a good many of them whizzing by before the crash.

One very impressive thing was the way about 20 seconds after one which set fire to a building about 2 or 3 blocks away, I heard a funny swishy noise start, and it was the pumps already at work! Marvellous! This sort of thing happened almost without a break till about 2.30 when I went to sleep. All very well for 1 night, in fact it was really an extremely interesting experience, but I have an increased admiration for those who live there. I caught a 6.30 train next morning. Having expected to emerge into a half-demolished street, I was amazed—and what was presumably the target [Victoria Station] was just the same as before, i.e., only some glass broken.

I am afraid this is rather a lengthy impression of one day, but I thought you would be interested.

I have been ploughing again this afternoon. We've got the thrasher in at last. The oat crop has turned out extraordinarily well but our wheat's turning out pretty poor, alas, there was too much charlock.

I wonder how bored you'll be by the time you've waded through all this. I'm exhausted I can tell you. It's midnight and I haven't yet brushed the dog.

COUNTRY DWELLERS

October 27, 1940

DEAREST H.:

We just got your letter written after your lovely birth-day party—what fun! Don't go feeling mean about it, or stop writing for fear of making us jealous, as it's fun hearing of nicer normal proceedings, and anyway, life's still pretty good, though not exciting or social. We've got J. here at the moment—arrived last night and he's going off again at crack of dawn tomorrow. I've taken a week-end's holiday as there's nothing v. urgent just at the moment, so J. and I had a long walk this afternoon. We had some time bombs dropped round here the night be-fore last—one's been found in the top of C—— field and they think there may be others—I don't know if they've been able to dismantle it.

I had a day of frenzied telephoning Friday as I'd ad-vertised a young pedigree Friesian bull for sale. To my surprise at least 6 or 8 people rang up to ask about him. There was the usual haggling—which I leave to F.—but we finally got what we were asking, £35—not bad.

Later. Soon after I'd finished this—a bit before dinner —there was a series of terrific crashes—we heard one of them whistle by, too. We all leapt far away from the windows and said, "That's the nearest we've had—not much more than a mile." A little while later we discov-ered what a very narrow escape Aunt D. G.'s had. There's a huge crater at the top of the field, knocking down her fence and a smaller bomb (they say the other may be a

[191]

mine) *just* missed the corner of the house, but great chunks came in, breaking masses of glass, knocking down chunks of plaster and unfortunately hitting a radiator and a w.c. cistern so that the whole place got flooded.

The crater—quite a small one—is actually where one of those yew trees was, the one nearest the house, just off the brickwork.

They wouldn't move last night, but the one thing they wanted was food, as their dinner was all out on the table and full of glass, so we took them up a basket of stuff and helped clear a patch where they could sit and eat it! They'll all be coming down for lunch and some of them probably stay.

Aunt D. G.'s really amazing—no flap at all—said she'd been sure she was for it within a day or two, had made all arrangements in case she had to evacuate, and was terribly relieved it was over and nobody even scratched. None of the damage will be really expensive. There were several more little ones within a ¼ of a mile, but no other damage, beyond a water tank, etc.

Did I say in my letter that there was no excitement! I thought as I wrote it perhaps that was not quite the right word. The Boche has lost £100 or 2 on that lot anyway!

F. of course was up there last night and I saw he had a large bit of plaster over a cut on the forehead. I asked him what had happened and he said, "I was trying to be helpful and walked into a beam!" The only casualty.

Well, I'll get this off now.

The following four letters are all from members of one family—the mother and two daughters, written to the mother's brother and his wife. This represents a typical Army-Church-small-landowning family. Every one of them is serving in some way, from the seventy-year-old father, patrolling as a Local Defence Volunteer, and the son who survived Dunkirk, down to the daughters working at the Ministry or growing vegetables. The tone of modesty and quiet devotion to their land is typical of this kind of family.

It will be seen that the son "M.," after a short leave, following the evacuation of Dunkirk, expected to be out again as soon as he was re-equipped. This was written before the fall of France, apparently, when the British troops expected to continue the fight in France.

BRECON
June, 1940

MY DEAREST G.:

We saw M. on Sunday, June 2nd. He had got back June 1st and was sent to Brecon for the night and off again next morning. He had been through a gruelling time, fighting practically continuously since the advance into Belgium and being among the last to be evacuated from the beach north of Dunkirk. He told us a thrilling story of his doings. He had lost everything, had not even underclothes on as they got so wet wading out up to his neck to a boat.

[193]

I won't write about it all—some day he'll tell you perhaps if any of us are left to tell anything. He was very full of heart and quite sure of the British infantry being very superior to the Boche. I expect he'll be out again as soon as ever they can re-equip. He hopes for 48 hours' leave but does not know.

L. [the husband of the writer] has joined the Local Volunteer Force and parades twice weekly and will be on duty nights, but not sure to what extent as yet.

I suppose it's hard for people across the water to realize things here—you do—but the newspapers are so awful and this is no European feud but a fight to the death for all that is most precious to mankind. I mustn't write about it.

J. will be interested to hear the vegetable garden is bursting with produce! I expect E. next week with 5 children. They left Kent. It was too risky—one air raid came very near. I can't think how we'll fit in or feed.

June 26, 1940

It is so impossible to realize what it is going to be like when it gets bad or indeed what the situation may develop into. . . .

I have now E. and her 5 children here. I have a great urge to depart and get into a munitions place but I must see them all comfortable and indeed I don't know where my duty lies. Light will come. M. is at H——. I think England is habitable to them after being abroad but I expect they'll be busy enough soon—all too soon. I've no news. I begged N. to go to you as her confinement is in Jan., when this island will be Hell, I expect, but she wouldn't hear of leaving and contemplates working to the last moment.

BRECON
July 15, 1940

MY DEAR J.:

I have very little news but you may both like to hear how we fare.

I have now E. and her family of 5 and governess, making us in all 15 in household. She lives near Folkestone and so more or less had to leave for the children, as raids were frequent. The house is very full and each of us has a child or so in our bedroom.

The garden is a wonder and now we pick peas and beans, etc., to feed 15. It is cram full of vegetables and we've dug more under the dining room and made it vegetables and also a big patch at the end of the lawn, so the children should get plenty this winter. I've worked very hard at it till my old bones ache! We are rationed all round but have ample of all things necessary; no one should complain—of course we live very simply. Sugar I try to save on so as to get more jam, but now there are 8 children, they have to have practically all.

You would be surprised by the war effort of our local roads. The village has 3 barricades and I suppose they are manned at night. E. has brought her car so we have 3 and the petrol ration is thus ample. I want to put one of ours up as an economy. To put into war savings is none too easy. M. is in Sussex in a very nice billet. He writes very little and says he is terribly busy. It is glorious to feel he is in the same land though it feels as though he was on another planet, one is so cut off from him.

The drawing room is packed up and turned into a schoolroom and the whole house is given over to children and always untidy and very muddy when it's wet!

Very much love to you both. A grand day is coming when we all meet again.

BRECON
July 19, 1940

MY DEAR J.:

Since writing you, your dear letter came so full of welcome to the family. I am so touched by your having arranged all and how I'd love to know they were safe with you. The transit seems a bit doubtful at present. I think C. feels that to leave H. would nearly kill her, but I expect it's very likely the time will come when at all costs she will want to get the children away. You can hardly realize the awful decision—at first I thought she was going to be really ill with anxiety.

Do you remember how you sang to me on my birthday, and it's just round again. This is the day we were to be invaded and it hasn't come off, so I can put in more cabbages tomorrow, I hope.

BRECON
September 5, 1940

DEAREST UNCLE G.:

Now I must tell you all the news of the family. Father is seeing life at Cardiff. The warnings there are continuous but the excites are mercifully over the docks. He is out all night once a week patrolling the road to Llanisham Station and seems to be at it most evenings too. He was here about ten days ago and seemed well in spite of it. M. is at or rather near Glo'ster in tents. He had 48 hours' leave last week and Mother went and joined Father and him and they had a bit of fishing in the Usk. He is to get 7 days' leave on September 25th if we are not invaded before then, and is coming here so we ought to have a real orgy then. K. and B. are at F—— and really in the thick of it. Warnings all the time and there have been bombs jettisoned at Leatherhead providing B. with heaps of casualties. But all is well with them, bless their darling hearts. Nothing seems to make P. leave London, she says now the warnings are so constant that they take no notice of them.

Since I started this letter we have had news on the wireless of the first bad raid on London. It is all so unutterably horrid and it's so beastly to be thirsting for news of Germany being dealt with even more faithfully by the R.A.F.

One of the most annoying things of life in this "beleaguered island" is that letters take 4 or 5 days to cross

it so that I get very little news of H. [the writer's hus-
band]. He is still at Folkestone or rather was on 31st
August, which was date of the last letter. He is getting
more prisoners to interrogate than he has time for and
complains of getting very little sleep. He's always liked
his sleep so that this will hit him hard.

Here, life is tremendous. Mother and I have got to the
point where we feel that any moment in which we are
not engaged in tilling the soil in the garden is definitely a
pause in which we are letting victory slip through our
fingers. It's a sort of frightful mania. But I believe sub-
consciously we feel like that because the garden is a
refuge from this houseful of children and one to which
they seldom penetrate. There are now 8 and all under
10, counting E.'s 5 and my 3, so you can imagine it.

And if P. comes here in December, it will be our third
confinement within the year! The one merciful thing is
that now I have Lucia I am much less cross and have
quite forgotten that I ever had a home of my own or
any snug place like that, so that life is far more liveable.

Mannie has now left agricultural implements behind
and is in aeroplanes. We have endless literature on identi-
fication of aircraft and he spends the mornings in the
oatfield to the north of the house spotting all that comes
over. Armstrong-Whitworths are his pet, there's a certain magic in the name I must say.

The 50 destroyers are cheering us all up no end, they
sound so snug and I hope Hitler simply hates them. The
Invasion season will probably be over by the time this

reaches you one way or other. I can't really credit the possibility, tho' I'm ever so alert morally and every other way, just as per instructions. Actually my only effort is to lay out the children's winter dressing gowns each night, where I can catch them up in the dark in case we have to rush below. But it's such a long way and the cellar stairs are so rickety that I'm sure the bomb would have arrived and exploded first.

The writer of this letter is an American married to an Englishman. Her son was invalided out of the Indian army before the war and got a job at Vickers', the big armament works. The story of how his mother took off the casualties from Vickers', after it had been bombed, not knowing whether he would be among them, is typical of what happens in England today.

The girl "A." who is referred to as being in the Air Force would be in the Women's Auxiliary Air Force. These women act for the Air Force as the Auxiliary Territorial Service act for the Army—as clerks, cooks and general odd-job girls.

SURREY
September 1, 1940

H., DEAR:

We are having very hectic days and nights but not nearly so frightful as the papers make them out to be. We have had a few bombs very near the house—one fell just near the station and just over the Golf Club bridge,

[199]

near the canal, four enormous bombs fell the other night. The craters are *enormous*, about 30 to 40 feet across, but luckily that is just swamp land there, not even any trees lost. Of course they were meant for Vickers, which isn't too comforting as my [son] G. is working there now. Poor boy, he has been invalided out of the Army and put on the half pay list (without pay) and after such a long time doing nothing he was glad to get a job at Vickers'. His Sandhurst engineering course helped him a lot. Also he was made head machine gunner in their Home Guard company, so he is getting on well and at *twice* his Army pay! Doesn't that seem unfair? He seems quite happy but I know he is terribly disappointed, especially as he seems perfectly fit.

I am doing A.R.P. work and drive my own car for sitting car cases—meaning I go out with the ambulances and take any casualties that are able to sit up in a car, to hospital. The only real work we have had so far was meeting the trains of wounded from France and Dunkirk. There has been no damage here.

I am sure you are longing for news and there is so much that I feel swamped. All the girls here have joined up. A. is in the Air Force. S. is like me, doing her own work and looking tired and weary.

Life, so far as occupation is concerned, has completely changed but otherwise everyone is leading the same comfortable peaceful life as before, with food plentiful (expensive) and the most glorious summer weather we have had for years.

September 14th. I wrote the enclosed about a fortnight ago—what ancient history it is now!

Since then we have had our real baptism of fire. Young G. was absent at lunch when we were called out to help with the casualties at his works, but I knew nothing of his whereabouts until after *hours* of carting the most heartbreaking casualties to hospital. It was a ghastly experience. We stood on the lawn and saw the whole attack—thinking it was our planes *practising* diving until we had to fly for cover! Then the agony of waiting for news of him.

Shortly after that, another lightning attack, when lots of incendiary and H.E. bombs fell on houses you know. Our old house had an incendiary on the tennis court and also the houses on either side.

J. had taken her grandchildren away the day before, but poor old S. was thrown out of his chair by a H.E. bomb that fell just by the tennis court and blew out all their windows. No other damage except that the drawing room, and S., were covered with soot! Quite a lot of damage was done to the W.'s house and you have seen what has happened to poor old London by the papers.

It is too awful to dwell upon but thank goodness we haven't the *time*. I have spent the past 48 hours doing all the windows with anti-splinter net. I have glued net on every window—all over it. After that day at the works it is obvious that flying splinters of glass is the greatest danger of all.

Young G. has had one or two very good "dog fights." Poor papa G. spends hours a day getting up and down from town and then most of his time in a shelter so he is more than "fed up."

I so often think of you and the anxiety you must be going through. I know you would rather be here, even with life as it is.

This letter is from an A.R.P. Group Controller in the country. A Group Controller had charge of the A.R.P. posts in the immediate district. A.R.P. Wardens warn the public of raids, report damage, give any help that is needed till the First Aid or Rescue Squad comes up, patrol the district for lighting offences, give advice on shelters—in fact cover almost every job that arises in connection with protecting the public against air raids. Some of them, working whole time, are paid. Others, working part time, are volunteers.

A "Red" is the red signal signifying that raiders are approaching the district. The yellow signal, which comes first, is not given to the public, only to the A.R.P. workers. Actual bombings are called "incidents."

BUCKS
September 22, 1940

It was my night off except for a Red or an incident (both of which happened). I'd just got to bed when off

went the Siren. I went down at once and stayed till the
All Clear and nothing happened, and then came home.
After about an hour I heard Planes overhead and then
one came low over our house and seemed to dive bomb
on G—— and there two H.E. bombs were dropped. I
at once dressed and went down again and everyone had
reported and was ready for anything. The Bombs were
both located—one in Whitefields allotments and the
other behind the Schools. One of the W.'s horses badly
wounded and had to be killed but no casualties. After an
hour all were dismissed and then a delayed action bomb
was discovered in French's (one of the First Aid party)
garden. The police evacuated all the adjoining cottages
at once and S., P., S—n and Mrs. R. were quite marvellous, getting old women, bedding, treasures, out of
the houses. No one knew at all the length of the delay
but thought it might be four or five hours. S. and P.
went back for some pet rabbits in the garden with T.,
and having got them out took them to a hutch on the
Abbey Yard and while there the bomb went off and
demolished French's cottage completely (in 1 hour and
ten minutes). They had been there 4 or 5 minutes before!! As I said, it was d—— plucky but b—— stupid. However, all is well and the police are most grateful for their
help and asked me for their names, etc. to thank them
officially. I am so proud really of all our A.R.P. now.
It functions so well and with little grumbling and so far
has had marvellous praise from above.

From a lawyer's wife in Edinburgh doing important work in connection with the Women's Auxiliary Police Force. This letter is included in the "Country Dwellers" section because it contains a good deal of country news.

EDINBURGH, SCOTLAND
October 9, 1940

DEAREST J.:

We are all right here, and although we have had a share of unwelcome attentions, of course it has been nothing like London so far. Everyone is dying to go there and help, but we can't. The epic of the people's bravery there is no doubt given in the American press. I have been amazed myself by the way the people in this town have behaved. The other night we had to evacuate several tenements because of an unexploded bomb, and one old couple who were hustled out of their home at a moment's notice were seen to be grousing like mad over something. On being asked what the matter was, they complained bitterly that the police by their action had made them miss the 9 o'clock news!

One finds that salvation in air raids lies in having something definite to do, and I am much sorrier for those who just have to sit in shelters and wait for the bangs. Travelling is most tedious and difficult, in that trains are often hours and hours late, but on the whole it is astonishing how little the country is affected—with the exception of London—and even there, they manage to carry on somehow with good humour and wit.

We sent P. and Ph. back to school in the end, and although they have to spend a certain amount of time in their shelters, they are able to lead more or less normal lives. When the sirens go in the daytime, they are greeted with prolonged cheers, as it means that the boys must stop work for a time. Of course I hate their being so far away, but after all, we are all in this whether we like it or not, and the risk is not much greater in one place than another, except in the big towns.

My parents have insisted on returning to Edinburgh in spite of all we could do. The first night they got back, we had three raids, but they didn't seem to mind.

I think your [son] J. had a very happy holiday. The three of them got lots of fishing and shooting and did some work either harvesting or with G. in the garden. Actually the farmers in that district seemed to have plenty of help, or the boys would have done more. There was only one contretemps when suddenly J. and Ph. lost their tempers with each other (over a small piece of cocoanut, believe it or not) and fought with some vigour until shamed into stopping by their grandmother hammering on the window of the library.

I have been seeing quite a lot of the Poles lately. They are enchanting and so dreadfully pathetic. They like the Scots and get on excellently well with them. My role has been dealing with the officers, practically all of whom speak either French or German, and I have taken them shopping and sight-seeing. The E. H's house in the country is a lovely hospital for them and we often go out there and spend a lovely evening doing music. They are intensely musical and sing beautifully. I found myself dancing a Mazurka one night, after which we retaliated by making some of the Poles dance an eightsome reel.

One good lady here wanted to entertain some of them and wrote to Capt. Z. asking for "The pleasure of his company" on such and such a date. When the day came, she was astonished to hear the sound of tramping feet outside her door, and there stood the Captain— *with* his Company!

I am so glad to think that you hear some good News Broadcasts on the short wave service from this country. The B.B.C. goes on here quite unmoved by what is happening outside and is the most steadying influence. I listened entranced to a performance of Hamlet during an alert, with John Gielgud, Celia Johnson, George Howe and the rest of a glorious cast. The ration for the sort of music one likes hearing is much reduced, naturally, but there is always something every day.

From a Women's Voluntary Services Organizer. The W.V.S. was set up before the war, when preparations were being made to train the public. This organization trained women for A.R.P., for First Aid and eventually for many other kinds of work, and so acted as a kind of clearing-house for women war workers. The W.V.S. co-operated with, and gave training to, many other estab-

lished organizations of women. When war eventually came, there were well-trained women all over the country ready to take over the job of organizing and carrying out emergency work.

LANCASHIRE
October 12, 1940

MY DEAR A.:

My job continues as before, and several of our "Canteen Shelters" (or refuges for the homeless) have been in use, most successfully. The workers have all turned up trumps and done magnificent work. I have over 400 of these places ready now in the country.

What a wonderful lot the R.A.F. are—where we should be if they were not so frightfully good, heaven knows. But the only thing now is to stick it out and wait till we are ready to take the initiative, which perhaps will come sooner than one expects.

I'm very glad you've got the children over there—it's no life for them here. It's pathetic to hear and read about the children in bombed areas—they are so frightfully brave—but I can't think it is possible for them not to be affected by it all—nerves and so on.

There is really little news to tell you, as life is very humdrum! One could do with a few more hours in the day, in order to catch up with things at home, but it seems impossible just now to have more than one day a week away from work.

We have received such a lot of gifts from U. S. A.

(goods and clothing) for homeless people, and I have to distribute a lot of it from our office. Each canteen shelter gets a certain amount, and the remainder is being stored at the Public Assistance Institutions and so on.

If I were you I'd wait a bit before coming back. There is no use in taking chances on the sea just now. The loss of the evacuee ship made everyone over here see red, and I don't think there are many Nazi sympathizers about these days!

My love, again. We often think about you so far away, but the Americans are such kind people I know they will be good to all of you.

II

"THE BACKBONE"

"THE BACKBONE"

If there is a common attitude in England today, it is largely because of the way in which the "backbone"— the people who always live on the narrow margin between safety and danger, whose income never quite covers all the needs of life—have endured the bombardment, remaining always grimly cheerful, prosaically gallant, and utterly contemptuous of their enemy. The thing that strikes one on reading these letters is, first of all, their humour, and, secondly, the writers' determination to go on leading their normal life in spite of all attempts to put them out of their stride.

Several of the letters are from Durham and Newcastle —towns in the industrial North, the home of miners, steel-workers, and cotton-mill operatives. The last letter is from Birmingham, the great munitions and machine centre.

The people of the North of England are very different from those of the South, where the rest of the letters in this section originated. Northerners are mostly stocky and short in stature. They are famous for their obstinacy, their taciturnity and their shrewd, rather grim humour. They consider the South to be rather too easy-going and frivolous. The Northerner lives in smoky and for the most part unlovely industrial cities and his countryside consists of lonely moors, mountains, and lakes.

The spelling and punctuation have been left uncorrected as it was felt that they helped to convey the flavor of the dialect.

The writer of the following letter is an ex-cook, 78 years old.

SCOTLAND
(undated)

MY DEAR SISTER:

I was glad to get your cheery letter and to know that all was well with you and yours. We are much as you left us. Of course we have been having the usual visit each night, and last Tuesday, he the perfect gent surpassed himself. You know the pictur house at the bottom of our Road, well all round there the damage was done. The shop where we get pork pies and further down, in fact I nearly got bumped out of Bed. I was like the man that had his belly slaped with the wet fish, it was a fright. Still my first thought was I am still here yet.

There was a good many got it a heap worse, so only for Windows being blown in we are still here to see it through. And as we say—"What do you know about That?"

The next day you should have seen our little old Village, you could not move for sightseers, and all our Friends came for miles to see if we were still on the

Map. What Ho! We still have our Thrills at my time of life. I will never be to Old not to be able to laugh at myself.

We had two Bumps, and the first one, E. came rushing downstairs saying—"we must go in the Cellar." I was cosy in Bed so I said just what you would have said "No, I'll no', Christmas!" The second bump helped me to make up my mind. We adjourned to the Kitchen and made some Tea, Bless Lord Woolton and John Haig.

Then E. went out to see what had Happened. The Electric was off, but there was an army of Working Men and all was calm and bright again. Next day Bizness as usual, and so the merry game goes on. I have seen for myself and it will take Old Lousy all his time to get us down, and then Some. He will never get us, so cheerio my dear, we are winning hands down.

Our B. came next morning. He came in smiling and I laughed too, because the daft thought came to me of E. coming down with his bit of hair standing up just like me.

M. had been to town for her First Aid lesson and had just managed to get the last Bus home, when she passed under the Plane that did the Damage. J. was worrying about her when she walked in. They got into the Funk-hole just in time. What a life, eh? We have just got notice (you know what I mean) Ten minutes later I resume. I feel very lonely now that you have

[213]

gone. Never mind my dear, we will have a holiday to-gether yet. Love to all of yours from mine.

Your loving sister, one of the ruins.

The following three letters are from two members of one family writing to a relative who is in domestic service in America.

The "shelter" referred to (which they had not got) would be an "Anderson" shelter—the corrugated iron hut which was issued free to people whose income was less than £5 a week. They were supposed to sink it half into the earth and cover the roof with a foot of soil. It was, however, only of use to those who had a plot of earth in which to sink it; others had to strengthen their cellars, or make do with the safest part of the house—as the writer of this letter describes.

"T. is on" means that T. is at work.

"Haw-Haw" of the letter of October 7th is of course the now famous broadcaster who pours propaganda into England from a German station.

NEWCASTLE ON TYNE
August 26, 1940

MY DEAR SIS:

Just a few lines hoping this finds you keeping well, as we are all fine at present. Your letter wrote on Aug 1st I received this morning. My word dear, you are certainly doing some knitting. I don't think I have ever

[214]

seen so much wool in my life. Bunty is never one moment idle, she has knit quite a lot now, for the Army
and Airforce, she is busy with a pullover just now, they
say she is a beautiful knitter and so quick at it. She has
also knit Joanie's little coats, also a winter coat and pull-
ups. I almost made a Balaclave Helmet. I done the
straight part and Bunty done the shapings. Bunt likes
knitting for the air force best. My but arnt they plucky
clever lads. They certainly have given *that man and his
cronies* something to think about.

I expect you will have heard they are over London
now. Well dear you were asking if we had a shelter, no
there is no room in our yard for one, so we go in the
cupboard under the stairs. Its almost as safe as a shelter.
Its a scream when you think about it, many a time
we sit and laugh, yet its no laughing matter when you
hear them over our heads. We get nicely settled in bed
when the siren goes and we have to run to our cubby-
hole, Pads and all, but it does not disturb Pads at all,
he curls himself up and snores. Night after night this
horrible siren goes, its got such a mournful weird sound
and we hear it so plain as its just above the picture
house. The all clear is quite different, its just one long
blast. Well dear let us forget it for a while. T. is on
ten till six this week, so I. and Baby come every after-
non and T. calls and has a cup of tea, then they go
home and have their dinner about 7.30. Wednesday
he starts six to two so they are bringing Joanie after tea

and they are going to the pictures, it is T.'s weekend off this weekend so they are going to I.'s cousin's wedding, they are taking baby with them. They wont stay very long. T. and I. bought her a Bolster set for her wedding present.

Its all so quiet at the time of me writing this. Bunt busy knitting, Daddy reading, Pads under the table asleep. Well dear cheerio and God bless you, Keep smiling.

NEWCASTLE ON TYNE
October 7, 1940

MY DEAR SIS:

Well now dear, I would just love you to walk in, laugh, you would scream. I have the whole of the table taken with the letters I have received from you this afternoon. Well dear, the letters I received today are dated Aug 29, Sept 1st which had the cheque in received safe and Sept 8th and the parcel the same day as Bunty got her letter. Many thanks for it, it was very acceptable, everything inside most useful and I am having the red dress cleaned, and Bunty is making me a jumper almost the same colour so I will feel quite smart for the winter thanks to you.

Bunt and I went down town this morning we generally go in the morning now, as I would hate to be in the town when there is an air raid, I like for all of us to be in the house when these air raids are on. Isnt it all too horrible, we have not had them so bad since they started on London, before they started London, we had them almost every day and night. Its terrible all those poor souls killed in London. Arnt our brave air force men giving them something.

Well dear this will be an encyclopedia by the time I am finished, I am going to answer all these letters I have in front of me. (If I can, there goes the siren) Bunt just said a few minutes ago she thought she heard A.A. fire.

You say in your letter you listened to Canada answering Haw-Haw, that Haw Haw had said the people of Britain were starving. My word, we are nothing like starving, there is plenty of everything, certainly we are rationed with some things but we get plenty of everything. When we were down town this morning, some shops were busy getting ready for Xmas. Xmas cards and calendars, and its looking quite like Xmas in there, in the market, it would make Hitlers and his gangs mouth water to see all the Butchers shops so well stocked.

Quite a lot of the places in the market are taken down, they are digging and making air raid shelters, they will be for the people that are in the market to go into when an air raid is on. Things are all dearer of course, and the purchase tax starts on Oct 21st.

Well dear here goes for another start, I cleared all off the table, the siren went nine oclock, all clear twenty past ten. There was some heavy firing, poor Pads when he hears the thuds, he looks at the window, then at the door, then he makes to the cupboard. So he and I went

in. Its now 10.30. I would like this finished and sent off
to you.

I am very well dear, touch wood. Have been for many
months now. I am glad you are keeping well, but dear
I wish you wouldn't worry so much. God's good, he will
see everything right in the end, and we long for the day
when we will have you home with us. Hitler is getting
more than he bargained for. Our Air Force are giving
him something to think about.

You will see dear that I am writing on the paper you
have been sending in all your letters, I could make quite
a nice pad with all you have sent. How nice of Mrs. F.
to buy a knitting machine. She has certainly worked
hard, and done a lot of good deeds, you are getting quite
a lot of knitting done. Bunt has got a Helmet and a
scarf finished, she will soon have the pullover done,
then she will take them in and get more wool for other
things. You would laugh if you saw me knitting, I have
done quite a lot, many an afternoon I never ly down, I
sit knitting, I have never knit so much in my life. There
goes the siren again, so dear I must finish this time, it
gives you such a funny feeling when it starts, its got such
a mournful sound, so dear dont worry we are all fine.
Keep smiling. Bunt says I have got to tell you the siren
sounds just like the New York Police, so Bye Bye dear
and God Bless you.

NEWCASTLE ON TYNE
October 31, 1940

MY DEAR AUNTIE:

Just a few lines hoping this finds you keeping well
as we are all fine at present. In your letter you asked us
to get you a pr of kid gloves. Mammy and I went down
town this morning and got them for you. We were in
a bit of a fix as to the colour. You didn't say what colour
you wanted. However we both thought you would want
black so we got you a nice black pair. I hope you will
like them. If they are not what you want, send them
back and we can change them. They said in the store
it didnt matter if it was three months after.

Mammy and I always go down town in the mornings
now. We went to get some silk stockings. There wasn't
any to be had under 5/11 and then there was just the
one shade. We told them to keep em. We'll have to
start and wear woolly ones like Mammy. She's certainly
got the laugh on us now.

Auntie, what could I send you for an Xmas box?
Would you like some new bedjackets? I have 2 nice
patterns. You wouldn't get them for Xmas of course.
Wouldn't it be nice if the war was finished for Xmas,
and we had you home. You know that the last 2 times
Mammy has wrote to you the siren has gone when she
was in the middle of it. You say in your letter Auntie
that you are very worried about us and what we must
be going through. Well Auntie, stop worrying. It really
isnt bad here. Its London that is getting it, not us. When

[219]

you hear that the North East has been bombed, remember the North East is a big place. There is no shortage of food, the navy is seeing to that.

Yes Auntie, "There'll always be an England" is a lovely song. No, we did not see any names on the American Ambulances. When we saw the 12 they went too fast to see any names. We saw one this morning. It was standing at the bottom of the Osborne Rd. It came from Newport Rhode Island.

T. and I. and I went to the Empire on Monday. We saw Geraldo and his band and Wee Georgie Wood. It was a jolly good show. It was packed. It starts at 3.15 and 6.30 now. We went at 3.15.

What a terrible night it is. It's pouring. T. will get soaked. He went on at 6 until 2 in the morning. Joanie is getting sweeter every day. She plays peekaboo with you now. I am going to buy her a Panda at Xmas.

Pads is washing his toes. Daddy cant take him for his walk at nights now as it gets dark so soon.

Cheerio and keep smiling.

A series of six letters from another family, in Durham, to a sister in domestic service in America.

The "siren suit" mentioned in the letter of October 30th is like a snow suit. All the shops blossomed out with them a month or two after the war broke out and they were very popular. They were, of course, intended to be put on hurriedly over nightclothes, and to keep the wearer warm in the cellar or shelter during a raid.

"THE BACKBONE"

DURHAM
July 11, 1940

MY DEAR SISTER:

I cannot tell you how thankful and relived I was to get your letters this morning. I got 5 altogether and I was glad to know you were well as I am glad to say we are at present also the family too. Although they seem to be having a very hot time on the coast. They have not got very far inland.

I hope you have been getting my letters. I did tell you we got more children this week, poor little mites they couldn't understand having to undress at bed time as they have been going to bed with half there cloths on one little girl was very slow in undressing so the Lady said come along. She said have I to take this off and this—various things. She said, wont we get an air raid tonight? She couldn't make out how she would not get up in the night. I tell the people here they dont know they are born. It will be a big mistake if they drop any here. But they are busy arn't they.

I expect you will have heard from both G. and L. they are having a very bad time. But I am glad she is near J. She says its not nearly so bad, she has company. H. says she would like her to go with them if they have to be evacuated. So goodness knows where we will all be before long. G. says they have there bags packed in case they get word they'll be taken inland a bit. I forgot to tell you Mrs. C.'s two boys are going to Canada. And M.'s boy of 7 and girl of 12 are going to U. S. A. They are going to friends, but they have not seen the children so its to be hoped they get over safely. Its wonderful how God has watched over the little one's that have gone over, and that the Germans torpedoed there own peoples ship wasnt that like them.

DURHAM
July 30, 1940

MY DEAR SISTER:

Again I take pleasure in answering your welcome letter dated 12th which I got quite safe this morning. Yes I got the paper cutting quite safe thanks. I see in the papers this morning the weather has improved perhaps its too hot for you now. Its a bit brighter now with us but nothing like summer the weather has been like the times lately. I expect A. wishes she was over here to see the baby. She wont be able to do so much for this one as she did for the others. I hope T. is better. I seen Mrs. C. a week past Sunday. They have sent there little boy to a place they used to be at but he does not seem to be settling so it would be no use them sending him abroad, would it.

Well now dear about your money, M. had £3.13 and some coppers so I told her to get a stove for the air raid shelter and I got 10/— for L. thats £2.10.0 she has of yours. I know you would not mind about the stove as when they have to go in sometimes twice in a night and getting out of a nice warm bed its not too good for the girls and I thought it best to let L. have the money as I dont know John's size. But will wait a week or two before I send it as she is at G.'s just now. And I have asked her if she will come up home, if not I will go down before the dark nights as it will be terrable traveling in the dark, you know the long weary time it takes. I do feel sorry about her as she did think J. was with her for a while however we will must just pray and hope for the best.

The Germans will stick at nothing to gain there cards, just you fancy sending Red Cross planes to do there dirty work. Its a wonder they are not afraid. They dont belive in any Higher Power so they wont think of any think coming to them. They have been busy lately but have lost a lot of planes. They are not getting things all there own way but it's the women and children that are getting the brunt of it and I see in the paper this morning that the invasion is off. They know they will be in for a bad time if they try that. We are well prepared for that. It wont be easy.

I dont know if I told you E. is in Hospital. He has been in since he got back from Dunkirk. I dont think he was wounded but isnt it a long time. They did have a time there. Who would have thought France would have given in like that. But theres one thing he wont get his tanks over here so easy of course we on the coast will have to be brave. But really, when I was home last week the people were wonderful. No panic at all. There's a family lives near M., 5 very young children. They just put the little ones to sleep in the air raid shelter and if they have to be disturbed the little ones know nothing about it. After one raid one of the little girls, shes 6, came in to M.'s I asked her if she was frightened she said No, Mummy said if you pray to God you will be all right. Wasn't that lovely. Well now dear I dont think I have any more to say this time. Again thanking you for all your kindness I will close with love and best wishes from us all I remain

Your loving sister

Good night and God bless and keep us all safe until we meet again I have not got your money sent to the red cross but will as soon as possible.

DURHAM
September 11, 1940

MY DEAR SISTER:

You will see that I am home for a week. I go back on Monday for a few days and come back home for good. And you will be surprized to know that I have L. and John with me. J. is somewhere in Scotland I think but hope to get home sometimes and its easier for him to get weekends.

Well dear I know you will be in a way at the news from this side this weekend. Its real war now. We have just had W. Churchill on the wireless. I expect you have heard him. Hasn't it been awful in London. L. says its been awful where G. is. John has brought us all a little bit of the parachute and cord that let down a mine into the creek. You know where the bairns used to go to bathe also a piece of shrapnel that wized past John's head when he was in the Harvest fields a few weeks ago. He has a great story to tell poor little lad.

Well now dear I wont stop to write more now only to let you know L. got here safe so hope this war will soon end we will wish you good night and God bless and keep us till we meet again your loving sister.

DURHAM
November 3, 1940

MY DEAR SISTER:

It gives me great pleasure to write a few lines hoping they find you quite well as it leaves us all at present. I expect you are all excited in U.S.A. with the elections. It will be a close fight by the reading in all the papers, wont it. I hope you have recived L.'s letter with E.'s letter in. I was asking W. about him being finished with the Army but he has not heard anything about it so the present would be something of there own as they are living with her father. I dont think she has a mother.

We have been very quiet since L. wrote until last night and then it only lasted ½ hour. G. had just gone to chaple. But they just carried on. Its wonderful how when the Siren goes all the bairns go to shelter and as soon as the all clear goes out they come to there play as if its nothing. I have been surprysed to see them. John loves his suit on. Thomas is home this weekend.

[225]

He goes back tody. But is coming home this next week-end for good. He hopes it wont be long before he gets a job. I dont think he likes being the only one away. But I think he has done well to stay so long, dont you.

Well now dear, I am glad you have such a nice place and hope you have got put right now. It takes some do-ing doesnt it. I have not heard from G. I expected a letter last week. They have had it pretty bad near them. Wont it be lovely when we are at peace again. I hear on the wireless that London had its quietest night since the blitz poor souls they wouldn't know what was the matter with them.

DURHAM

October 30, 1940

MY DEAR SISTER:

Well, dear, here I am at last. I might have written befor, I know but you know how it is with a crowd. And J—e has written and given you all the news. Well Dear, I am glad to say we are all keeping very well for all the to-do's we are having but its marvellous the way one keeps on the go.

The children are wonderful. All that seems to worry them is getting out the morning after and who can find the most shrapnel. John has a grand collection and lass, you should see him in his "Siren Suit." You know J—e told you we made it out of your Green Coat. It is very cosy and warm. I wish I had that bit coat you sent me up here. It would have been just the thing for the shelter. We were in about 4 hrs on Monday night and mind its grand to hear our guns peppering them.

J. was home for the weekend so we had a nice time. He hopes to come again in a month then it will be Xmas leave. I hope he has a long stay up there as its handy for him to get here for a wkend. John gets on A.1. at the Newtown school and has quite a lot of Pals. Edwin stayed here all last week the schools had holiday. G. had her holiday so last Wednesday we all tripped up to N—— to see the Pictures. Its wonderful to see the crowds still. J. just said on Saturday when we went round the town you wouldnt think there was a war on. All the same I wish it was all over and we could get settled down again. I am pleased to say I left G. and all quite well but I think they have had a very warm time of it lately. You see they are in what they call the "Thames Estuary." E. had been home but went back the week after I came home. Winnie was fine but G. didn't like her coming home in the blackout. Two Jerries had been brought down near G. last week.

Maggie and Ella have just been in. They are off to N——. Ella wants a hat, etc. Fenwicks Bazaar opens today and John had been over to Maggies this morning giving orders. He's a lad. I'm afraid he'll not want to go back to quiet Suffolk after this lot is over. He and Marjorie are very good pals and when they come over on a Sunday he puts Dinky curlers in her hair and doesn't she like it. She is a funny little thing and so fat. John calls her tubby but he can't say much. He's in good condition. I usuall call up there every Thursday when I go for my money and stay to tea and sometimes supper, then W. walks down with us. Gladys is coming here to tea tonight. My she's a great big girl and getting on well.

Now dear we had this letter come this morning from E. J—e is sure you won't mind her opening it. They seem very grateful for the present. They were a lovely pr. of sheets. He has been in hospital a lot since the Dunkirk do. With his stomach. J—e was very pleased to have your welcome letter this morning. Of the Oct. 13th. She will answer it soon, only she wrote yesterday so I said I would write today for a change. The weather today is awful. Wind and rain and so cold. So we are keeping the fire warm. I had a letter from Jack this morning and he got back safe but I hear on the wireless they are having a warm time but he is very cheerful. I'm glad you were able to hear Princess Elizabeth. She was lovely and I think she speaks exactly like the Queen. I do think they are all so splendid.

Well dear I really think this is all the news I have this time so with every good wish from us all I will close. Ever

Your loving Sister

Lots of love and x x x to Auntie
from John

Good night and God bless you Dear.

DEAR AUNTY:

Once again I take the pleasure of writing to you. I hope you are keeping fine as all at home are just now. A few weeks ago Mam and I went to the pictures to see Hollywood Calacade I enjoyed it but Mam wasnt so struck with it. Last Monday we went to see "Its A Date" with Deanna Durbin I was disappointed and expected something better. It was showing at the Odeon, that was the Paramount you know but it is under new management now. You would wonder where all the people came from you wouldn't think there was a war on.

Well now aunty, we have had a good many visits from Uncle Jerry and his friends lately but he can't damp our spirits take it from me (straight from the horses mouth). We expect him every night now because every night last week he gave us a visit but mind you give him his due he came about 9:45 so you see we weren't in bed and had not to be awakened from our sleep. For all the times he has been over and the bombs he has dropped he has not done much damage. He has hit no military objective in our quarter. There was a few bombs dropped in —— Street only a few houses were knocked down and one person killed and a few injured. Mam has got the shelter nice and comfy. She has managed to get a standing bed in so Gladys and I sleep in now all night. We never hear a thing as we generally go straight to sleep.

Mam just lies on the bed in the shelter so we rely on her to give us the news when we wake up in the morning. Mam does not stay in the shelter all night with us when the warning goes she comes down stairs and goes back to bed again when the all clear goes. We don't half pepper our guests when they do come, the tinkers, I can tell you. Doing the shelter in the mornings and getting it ready at night is all in the day's work now. The door step is not the last thing you have to do before you are finished the mornings work but the air raid shelter. It is laughable to hear the neighbours say what they want and what they are going to get for the shelter it is just like furnishing another room of their house.

Well we are getting on fine with our tap dancing and keep fit. Gladys has made herslf a dress at the club and it does look nice. We will soon be having an experienced dressmaker in the family. She has started to make a pair of Gloves but I won't say when they will get finished. Thomas is keeping fine and is still away.

Huh, what do they think we are over in Germany. Hitler wants us to let him have 64 red cross boats for his airmen round-a-bout our coasts. By his crack he has only lost a few planes and men. I expect the small boats would be observation or small torpedo crafts they must think we are green. Everyone in the Country are wholeheartly in harmony fighting Hitler to blazes. Thats right Aunty you just go nineteen to the dozen when they start over there about us.

"THE BACKBONE"

From the seventy-year-old proprietor of a small seaside boarding-house.

HERNE BAY, KENT
September 21, 1940

DEAR I.:

. . . I live very quietly here and don't go about. One (I do) feels it is safer to remain near to ones home. We get plenty of liveness from the sky I can assure you. It is quite safe to watch because our Aviators force the Jerries out over the water mostly, and from there engage them in deadly combat. It's a most wonderful thrill to see them tumbling down, sometimes in flames and the crew baling down gracefully in their Parachutes. Nought like it in America! Some poor Devils cant get out and are buried in their machines, or smashed to bits.

HERNE BAY, KENT
September 24, 1940

MY DEAR I.:

There is a huge excitement on from the Air. Masses of German planes have crossed and our Aviators have forced them out over the water, engaging them in dog fights and they are tumbling down like ninepins. It is better than the Pictures! A real thrill!

We are very lucky here. No casualties or damage. Only bombed once by a lone raider. He dropped two bombs—one fell in soft garden ground and the other through the roof of "Grand Hotel" near station; only

[231]

making a small hole about as big as the base of a large cottage loaf.

It is very dull here apart from the fun in the air. Half the shops and houses are empty; although both the cinemas open daily until 10 P.M. I never go though.

Hitler seems loath to invade us but I wish he would, and quickly. It would be better for us to defend our Island than to set out to retake the Countries off him again that he's grabbed. The time's going on and the winter will soon be here. It gets dark here now (Summer Time) about 7.30 P.M. I dread the long dark nights. We do not put Clock back until mid. Nov.

Goodbye now, with love to you both. No need to worry about me. All is well apart from a wee bit of rhumatism. I'm going to knit a heavy wool Cardigan, so that will provide interest.

From a Birmingham mother to her son in the Royal Air Force, who enclosed it in a letter to a friend in the U. S. A.

BIRMINGHAM
November 20, 1940

DEAR SON J.:

Its my Birthday today 64 my Second war. We have no windows in one room, no gas, and a beautifull Shower Bath is waiting outside. But we all went to Bed Cheerfull. And got up thankfull. a Bomb dropped in B—— St. made us *all* turn over. heart included. J. was on guard at the mint they missed it and Hit next door we are all O.K. dont worry I am packing some things today in the large traveling case and having it put in the celler. Things were certainly very bad here last night everyone had to be evacuated from B—— Street. But Belive me, every one *man woman* and *children* too are never heard say, *Stop it,* all they clamer for is more action, all ask the Chance to *fight.* Everyone here says they were Italian Plains that came over last night. It is 7 oclock S. has just been, all his doors and window frames have been Blown in. C—— Rd. has been Cleaned up all together. Houses everywhere are down if it keeps up like this I'll go to E.'s. She told M. to ask me to go to Her. She is worried about me I'll think it over. M. removed to B—— on Friday. She has a good Shelter. Then I'll see what M.'s is like. She has removed and they have 3 good cellers. You know they had to crouch under the stairs. The house is a large one and she has a big garden She can grow things in. If a Bomb drops in they will make a duck Pond. They Bury the Coventry people today. above 200. Dont worry. I'll go. But where the Hellenor *too* I dont know. Thats all. Best of love and God Bless you from your ever loving mother and all at home.

Did you get those parcels let me know. If you write J. tell her and the children I send my love. And that we are all in the front line.

III

THE OLDER GENERATION

THE OLDER GENERATION

Two letters from a lady of well over seventy who has perfect physical health and is an active Air Raid Warden. The first letter describes the perils through which her son, who was on the G.H.Q. staff, passed during the evacuation of Dunkirk. The second describes her sensations and impressions when the raids on London begin.

CHELSEA, LONDON

June 3, 1940

MY DARLING ONE:

Thank you for your lovely sympathy about my B. Last week was quite shattering: there was so terribly little chance of the survival of any of G.H.Q.—the enemy making that their special goal—and they were bombed and harried without ceasing, this last 3 weeks, and had to be continually changing their position, and all the time of course dreadfully anxious about the troops and whether they would get through the corridor to the beaches of Dunkirk. B. had no time to sleep during all these days—ceaselessly working out plans to get them out. Their rearguard fighting was an epic of skill, confidence, discipline, and marvellous fighting qualities and bravery. I loved to hear him speaking of them today. He came up with [his wife] to go and replace the whole

[237]

of his wardrobe and equipment as, in the end, it was a case of leaving just in the garb you stood up in. And to get to a sort of flat boat (or raft) that he saw in the sea, he had to wade nearly neck deep for a quarter mile and being attacked all the time from the air. He scrambled on somehow, together with a few men who were already on the beach, but who had not thought the raft (or craft) looked nearly safe enough to cross in—but when he said he meant to try for it they went too. Then after some time on this perilous affair, an amateur yachtsman hove in sight, saw that he could help and took them in tow, but, as B. said, "his bits of string kept on breaking" and he seemed to know nothing about "navigation" or even tying knots that would stay tied, and then started his motor with a slack line and a great dash, breaking everything of course! All this under enemy bombardment. Finally, after incredible adventures, a destroyer picked them up and all was then well. I had a lovely time today with him, and N. came up so we were all happy together. I must stop now, but will write more soon.

CHELSEA, LONDON
August 26, 1940

DARLING ONE:

This just to let you know that I am all right, as you will have read of all the raids here, and of course I am in my element, and really enjoy my work here, although it is, of course, very strenuous.

Saturday night we had a succession of raids lasting all night. Very thrilling. I've never seen anything as beautiful as the sky that night, and on top of this the loveliness and mystery of the attacks and the gorgeous searchlights focussing on the planes with marvellous accuracy. The bridge was the centre of dozens of lights, mostly vivid blue. The crews seem to have got them perfect now, and they are an enormous help in the Defence. Of course all the guns were going, and the noise of them was terrific.

A huge fire broke out in Aldersgate in the City, and turned all the sky in that area a deep rose colour, with shoots of flames at intervals. It was all so beautiful but so satanic. We expect more raids in the near future. We have had 2 more on Sunday, and one already today, two during last night. The first sirens caught me in my comfortable bath, and I leaped out, and half dry, flew into my clothes. How quickly one can dress, from A to Z, in an emergency. In 12 min., I was out complete in uniform.

It was very dark last night, the moon now so very late in rising, so no good. The Jerries seem to be "getting the wind up" at our R.A.F. boys' daring. No wonder, poor devils. One hopes that this feeling will develop into real panic, and the Nazi will refuse to go up.

From a schoolmaster's wife in the north of England, to her son.

June, 1940

The great trouble of these days is the young people. None of them can make plans as they would like, because the war comes to upset plans and to part loved ones from each other. As far as we can see, all this cruelty looks like dragging on indefinitely.

We get very little news except war news, and hardly know how the rest of the world is faring. It seems hard that now that we have war conditions, there is little unemployment. Lancashire is on the way to a boom period. There are not enough weavers to turn out the necessary orders, and wages for cotton operatives have risen 20 per cent since September. Of course, that is a move in the right direction, but it is deplorable that it is only because of the war that this is happening. People whose shops were stocked with goods are making money fast. Mothers and wives whose husbands and sons have been called up are the ones who are suffering mentally and financially.

News seems to grow worse day by day. It is with deep sorrow that we listen to the tale of bombing and murder, and the wastage of innocent young life. For so many mothers there are long times of waiting without news of their sons. N. had just got his B.A., and had to join the army at once. He was in France, and for a long time his parents had no news of him. His mother saw a picture of him in a paper, along with others who had been evacuated at Dunkirk. Next morning she had word that he was safe in England!

Holidays in Lancashire cotton towns are being postponed till the end of August, so we may not get any.

From another mother.

SOUTHAMPTON

July 3, 1940

Don't worry about us, my dears. You have your lives to live and if the end comes suddenly to us—well, console yourselves with the thought that we have had 45 years of the happiest married life, which is much more than most can say, and we have the satisfaction of knowing that, as far as we can tell, your future, and your brother's, we hope, is secure. We have arranged for you to hear by cable if anything serious happens, so don't get alarmed if you hear reports of bombing at Southampton, and if you *don't* get a cable you will know we are all right. It's surprising how accustomed we get to hearing guns, etc. I help with the canteen, also we are busy jamming and bottling surplus fruit—the Women's Voluntary Service have taken over the disused school and we have had sugar released especially for this purpose. We are making thousands of pounds of jam in this way so that the fruit shall not be wasted.

Two letters from a great-aunt of 80. "Uncle T.," who is mentioned herein, is 83; "Aunt L." is 90.

DORSET COAST
July 16, 1940

MY DEAR L.:

I was so pleased to get yours. You must be in your element enjoying the pure air, the lovely wild flowers and the birds and doing a bit of gardening.

Well, L., I am glad to say we are all well, even though we are living in a very anxious time, each morning wondering what will happen before the day is over. The raids are very alarming, especially at night when you have to get out of your warm bed to go to your shelter. All we can do is to trust, believing and knowing our Heavenly Father is watching over us and He will bring us safely through this terrible war, for Right must prevail over Might. I hope you won't risk coming back to England until things are very much better.

We had a cable from G. a few days ago asking us to send two children. It was very kind of him. We would like C.'s youngest girl and M.'s boy to go but the Government has stopped sending children at present on account of the difficulty with the boats.

N. has joined the W.A.A.F. She is doing canteen work at present. She is at St. Albans, she may be removed to London. We have not seen her since Easter. J. has joined the signalling branch of the Navy, and C. is in the Air Force.

Aunt L. keeps very well. I spend every Wednesday afternoon with her, we have a very happy time together.

She loves to talk about the young days, she has a marvellous memory. She sends her very kind love to you. Uncle T.'s sight is very bad, he can't get about like he used to, it is upsetting.

I think I have written quite a long letter. I am feeling rather tired, we had two warnings last night, that meant going down stairs twice in the middle of the night. I hope we shall have a quiet night tonight, but we don't know. I rest by day but I can't sleep.

DORSET COAST
August 26, 1940

MY DEAR L.:

I was so pleased to get your letter of the 4th instant. I feel I know that Our Heavenly Father's Boundless Love is now taking care of me and my dear ones. We are passing through troublesome times, but we have much to be thankful for, we are not short of food, we have enough and to spare, and everybody seems cheerful and looking forward to better times, which I trust will come soon.

You see by the papers how wonderful our Airmen are. They are doing grand work and they are not getting weaker but stronger every day.

We have had a wonderful summer. The flowers, trees and sunsets have been marvellous but we can't enjoy these beautiful things as we should because of the war.

[243]

Well I am a great-grandmother. My great-granddaughter was born on the 19th. I am pleased to say Mother and baby are getting on very nicely.

Aunt L. is fairly well. She is feeling the effects of the air raids but she is very wonderful. She will be 90 Sunday week.

From two aunts, to a nephew in America. The first writer is 85, the second 86. Norfolk is on the east coast, which was under fire for many months before the rest of England began to be raided.

NORFOLK
September 11, 1940

MY DEAR T.:

I was so glad to get your letter. Thank you for it. Such a nice long one too, it ought to have been answered before but writing letters is getting a bit difficult for me now, and I have rheumatism in my right arm which does not improve matters, but it is not very bad and I can still get about well and do nearly all my own work, so must not complain. No, I have not had to evacuate I am thankful to say. We have had bombs dropped in W—— less than ½ mile from me but no casualties and very little damage. It is a terribly anxious time but I am not at all nervous, the poor Londoners are suffering now but that brute Hitler is not going to have it all his own way and his defeat will be complete. It seems terrible

[244]

that one man's ambition should cause all this pain and suffering.

I am so glad you are all well and F. and K. too. I will write to them as soon as I can. Aunt N. is well and is going to Bristol, I hope to live. Aunt M. has had to leave Y——, it has been often bombed, and has locked up her house and with her sister gone into rooms at F——. She says she is quite comfortable, but it is sad to have to leave one's home like that.

I wonder how you are getting on about the children you expected. I hope it is comfortably settled by this time. How good to read that K. has bought a house and how nice of him to call it that name. I should dearly love to go to dear old W—— again, but dare not hope for that now. I expect C. has not been able to get over to England this summer as he hoped to do, he promised to come and see me if he did. I do so wish you were all in England and could come and see me now and again. I had loving thoughts of Daddy on the 9th of this month. You must not mind if I don't write for your birthday for I have lost my Birthday Text Book and can't remember any dates now. My age affects me more in the matter of memory than in any other way. We are having a very cold month and I had to begin fires the day before yesterday though not till I sit down in the evening.

Both this and my other house next door have had to be painted and done up this year. This one is finished and they are at work next door now. I wish I could get my garden done, but labour is so short now. I can't get anyone to come and do it, and it is beyond me now. I don't at all like not being able to do as usual.

How do you think the war is progressing? Hitler is getting desperate at our resistance.

Now good night, much dear love to one and all. Write again as soon as possible to

Your loving Aunt ——

HERTS
August, 1940

MY DEAR T.:

Poor Aunt K. has been bombed out of her home. Her bedroom ceiling is down, there is a hole in the roof, and all the windows at the back of the house are shattered. She has gone to E. at W——, but will go back when the house is declared to be safe and can be protected from the weather.

Like you I am late at night—12:30 A.M. into bed is my usual time, and the other night it was 2:10 A.M. due to air raids about, when you hear bombs dropping all round. Consequently, I suppose, I find myself sometimes dropping to sleep even in the middle of whatever I may be doing—meals not excepted! But I am well and busy—think of me sawing and chopping wood in the garden or shed: not bad for an old party of 86.

Our food bill is interesting:

Lemons—6d. each—we have 1 a fortnight.
Fresh eggs—4d.—we don't have any.

Loaf sugar—not to be had.
Granulated sugar ½ lb. each for everything, cooking in-
  cluded.
Butter—2 oz. each per week—4 oz. margarine.
Tea—2 oz. a piece per week.
For want of sugar our cooking-apple harvest is of little
  use to us.

*This letter is from the "Aunt H." alluded to by the
farming girl in Sussex, in the "Country Dwellers" section.
Here that same girl is referred to as "B."*

SUSSEX
September 21, 1940

DEAREST H.:

Just a line to send you every best wish for your birthday, next Saturday, and to apologize for being late. I have
been meaning to wish you happy returns for more than a
week but have always forgotten to ask your address when
I've seen your Mother and B. It has been very nice getting news of you through them.

You will know all our news from the papers and your
Mother and B., Aunt L. and all your friends on this
side. I expect you would really like to be in England in
these momentous days and will regret not having been
in the thick of things here.

While I am writing I hear enemy planes overhead and
a bomb has just dropped quite close I imagine as it has

shaken the house—and now your Mother, B. and Br. have just walked past on the road—I dashed out and found that they of course had heard the bomb and the planes were still passing high up over our heads above the clouds but making their usual droning noise—I expect they are making another week-end mass attack on London—we hear them every night now and sometimes in almost continuous waves for two or three hours.

Your family were trying to warm themselves by walking as fast as they could as it is such a raw day. I expect Aunt L. has told you about the enemy plane which was shot down last Sunday and fell on the roof of a house just opposite her kitchen window and how excited and interested M. and F. were and the 2 other guests who were lunching with her that day.

I am afraid thousands of poor people in the East and near the docks have had their homes destroyed.

I am so thankful the King and Queen were not hurt in any of the raids on Buckingham Palace. It was awfully nice when that working man called out the other day, "You are a great King," and he instantly replied, "And you are a great people." I love the thought that we are being "Honored by destiny." The deeds of heroism that are taking place every day and every night are simply marvellous! I think perhaps the most outstanding bravery of all is that of the people who dig up unexploded bombs when sometimes for three days on end they may be blown up at any moment.

Ever so much love and all best birthday wishes and kindest remembrances to your Uncle and Aunt.

From an English lady who had to take refuge in England after France fell.

DERBYSHIRE
October 24, 1940

MY DARLING:

A fortnight ago you wrote to me! It doesn't seem so very long ago and I can tell you my relief was immense. I thought my answer to your previous letter could not have reached you and that perhaps I should not hear again and another tie be snapped. This appalling cleavage between the old life and the new needs all one's strength to bear, but we must struggle on on our new hard road and not lose our vision. Injustice and wrong cannot prevail in the end, but whether we old people will live to see a better world remains to be decided. I try to think we will, and be once more reunited. Bear with the present, bad as it is. You have your job which is a grand good thing and will keep you sane till better times come along. And who knows, perhaps some day we may all be reunited in our loved Paris—let's hope a Paris cleansed of all that rabble of despicable traitors. Or perhaps you will be able to get over to England or to some free country and we shall remember the many heavenly days we spent together.

I feel very lonely here and my black moments are like

yours. Everything then seems futile. This is an ungrate-
ful, cowardly spirit, I know, specially as I have countless
things to be glad and thankful about. As things material
go, we are of the luckiest, for we are here in a perfectly
peaceful village. Poor London! and poor many other
places, but the people stick it and nowhere is there any
thought of giving in. What are the feelings over with
you? We could achieve much with U. S. A.'s endless re-
sources, but it will take time and meanwhile our mar-
tyrdom must go on and we must stand alone.

As a family, so far we have not suffered. A. is back at
the University, and the town where they live has had a
raid but come off lightly. They have kept the caravan
so as to dash out and see the little boys when A. is free.
T. was in an awful spot with the roughest and most illit-
erate of companionship. He has now been put into something quite different and bumps up against interesting
people. Of course he is only a private. We have seen him
lately. It seems funny to see T. busily engaged making
his boots shine, cleaning his buttons, etc., he who was
so *peu pratique*. I am glad he is serving where he is as it
is interesting. In his last job he learnt all about motors
and drove huge lorries. He looks very well. I simply dare
not think of the future—if we do come through, what on
earth is a child like T. to do? His studies all interrupted
after a year at Oxford. In his present life he has not a
minute's time for study and if we do come through it
will be years and years of training for a career. However,
I must not grouse. He is alive, anyway, up to now, and

there are hundreds of young fellows in just the same position, so away with *cafard*.

From another lady of 76.

S.W. ENGLAND
September 15, 1940

Just a few lines, my dear, to let you know we are still in the land of the living in spite of Fritz. Not much excitement here. One cracker made the tea cups jump one day but the old home is having quite an exciting time as they generally get turned back from there and if they are in a hurry generally unload in the district but very few casualties.—There is a lot of open ground about fortunately.

It is difficult to prevent people gathering to see the dog fights and so make casualties of themselves—personally I'd love to be on the cliffs to see what is going on. There is a funny side to it all—one old lady was too old to be moved to shelter. As soon as the "all clear" had gone, her grandson ran in to her to find her smothered in mortar, glass and dust. The old lady looked up and said, "Just dust off this rubbish, Billy, and I'll go to sleep again."

Really, the people are wonderful. The Anderson shelters are quite a success.—They have just finished a very good one for this hotel.

Did I tell you F. was ordained a Benedictine on July 22nd? I did not go up as traveling is slow these days. T.

did not go either. They too have crackers—one or two old people departed from shock. F. and his mother have been staying in Oxford—F. having three weeks' holiday. He looks terribly tired and M. got the flu and had to go into nursing home. Is there still. Bad luck as she only sees F. once a year. I wonder if you could send me 1 lb. China tea or one Indian. I do hate hotel tea and long for a cup in my room but being rationed, Hotel takes coupons. I will find out and let you know as I am not sure if I would have to pay more duty than it is worth. I like Lipshong, Oolong, and Shoolong China, if you can get it and any really good Indian.

D. is still doing A.R.P. work. He is really wonderful and so pleased to be making a bit on his own. Poor old thing. Says he sleeps through all air warnings so that does not worry him. Chin, my peke, objects to Fritz dropping crackers. Gives a most vicious bark at nights.

We are having the most wonderful weather. We are trying to get a small 2nd hand car. I find walking to church two miles is really a strain on an old lady.

We left the big one at home as it used too much petrol. Want one just to run around in. One man came home on leave, bought one for £5, did Scotland—Ireland—lovely holiday. Had to hurry his departure. Nearly missed his boat so left car on quay. Two months after in India received letter to say would he kindly remove it. Second letter to say unless he moved it would be sold and he would be fined. Third letter to say it was sold. They had deducted his fine and they enclosed a check for £25. So he did well.

This hotel is full of evacuees like ourselves. Some from Jersey. They left in a hurry. Just wrote B. Do you see any English paper? Would you care for "Weekly Times"?

IV

DECISIONS AND CHANGES

DECISIONS AND CHANGES

In ordinary times, women do not very often have to take life-and-death decisions: but when this war broke out, thousands of women were immediately faced with the need to make such decisions—decisions which, once taken, might affect the whole of the rest of their lives, or of their children's lives. Most of them concerned the question of evacuation; whether it was better to split the family between the generations, the wife remaining with the husband and sending the children away, or to split it lengthways, as it were, so that the children should have at least one parent with them. When evacuation was decided on, the place had to be chosen. There was also the question— "Have I the courage to stand it, if I do stay, or shall I serve my neighbours and my family better if I take my not-too-sound nerves away where they can disturb no one?" and, "If so, shall I hate myself all my life and live under a shadow that makes me unbearable to everybody?"

The necessity for making such vital decisions, often under the pressure of danger and bereavement, has been one of the major stresses of this war. The following eight letters show the various ways in which different women replied to offers of homes for themselves or their children from friends or relatives in the United States. The third of these letters (page 260) is from an Englishman's

American-born wife, whose mother has urged her to come back to the U. S. A., where her three children happened to be at the outbreak of war.

HERTS

July 3, 1940

MY DEAREST C.:

You can imagine, I expect, the agonies of mind we have been going through since your first cable reached us. We are so very grateful for your thought of us, and always *shall* be, whatever the outcome of our present decision may be. (*That* is the hardest part of all: shall we one day wish to God we had decided otherwise?) If M. had been coming actually to your house, I think we should have felt the advantages overweighted everything—but only just! And if it is to strangers, however kind and generous, I feel we just can't. We had to weigh up the certainty of losing touch with him just at the age of puberty, when he needs home most; and the certainty that his education would be interrupted with a jerk (however excellent the new school) just as he has won a big scholarship to Ampleforth; and the probability that he would find it very hard to fit into either the educational or the social scheme of things in a puzzling post-war England, a year or two hence—all this against the possibility of his being killed or damaged by the war. A *frightful* choice to have to make, C. May you never have to go through it. It has added twenty years to our ages. But we do want you to know how grateful we are for all your thought for us and him. We have promised him that after the war he shall go to the States on his own for a holiday—perhaps that may be sooner than we fear.

G. and I have just been snatching ten days' holiday. Cars being things of the past, we went to Stratford-on-Avon on push-bikes taking three days on the journey, and stayed there for five days (seeing five plays at the Memorial Theatre) and then cycled back. It was very good fun, and did us oceans of good. We had not been off on our own for ten years!

RADNORSHIRE

July 16, 1940

MY DEAR J.:

It is sweet of you both to offer homes to the family and just like you. We can't begin to thank you. Sending the "brats" away had never even come in to our heads but since getting your letter we tried to think clearly and weigh things up, with this result. We feel, in the country and not near the coast, that it is best to stay put. As you know, we don't see many folk about here, but judging by the papers our tails are well up all over the countryside. Here what little influence we have is being used to help this corner of England to keep its tail up. What sort of an example would we set if I flitted with the Brats? This is not trying to magnify my importance in the scheme of things. If we were living in a congested or coastal area we would surely have sent the children away from it, with or without me as circumstances ordained, and no one would have missed us. We would have been one invisible drop in a vast ocean. Here no. We feel it would be wrong and would undo all our "Don't worry but get on with your job" campaign.

I feel so much sorrier for you than for us! It sounds daft but we are in it and you are such a terribly long way off. Granted Belgium was a bit grim and France a bit grimmer just when we had got over Belgium, but now there's just us. Call us British Empire or British Commonwealth of Nations or what you will, but "being of one mind in one house." I haven't got that quotation right, but anyhow we are possessed of one very determined determination. . . .

KENSINGTON, LONDON
May 30, 1940

MY DARLING MOTHER:

You know that there is nothing I want more on this earth than to come home, and it was one of the hardest things I have ever done to cable that I would not take the passage on the *Roosevelt*, but I just could not do it. I wouldn't be your child and Daddy's, if I lit out now—when things are dark. I don't want to be killed any more than you want me to—and you can be sure that I will take every precaution possible and not run any risks, but I must stay here. It is all very grim and heart-breaking now. But I am sure that it will come right in the end. We shall have some pretty black times first and horrid things will happen. But if you are being busy and doing things you get along. You can't think how wonderful it is to know the boys are with you, and out of all the mess.

P. and B. both thought London was better for the present, so we came pattering back again. And we are now doing Surgical Dressings every day—so I don't have much spare time.

Even now we go on just the same. Last night I went to the theatre with T. and enjoyed it very much. I hoped P. would get home tonight but he has just rung up to say that he isn't going to be let off. They are moving them again tomorrow. He has moved so many times, poor dear. However, he will still not be far from here.

Poor A. is feeling very blue because she may have to be interned. I tell her that it's just the fortunes of war and that it is much better to be in a British camp than a German one. I shall miss her dreadfully if she has to go but I think it is right. Not that I suspect her but we can't take any chances with these buzzards.

Don't worry about me any more than you can help. I know it is hellish for you, and I wish I could do something to make it easier, but I can't run away now. We are all very calm and go on just as usual. Don't think we live in a panic or a gloom because we don't. I must say, I feel a new woman when I have my nightly Old-fashioned.

EDINBURGH
June 6, 1940

DEAREST R.:

It was angelic of you to offer to have the children. About the older boys, I agree with O. and P. in thinking that one ought not to send them out of it unless many, many others do. They would never forgive one later. And it would be awful for them if people said, "Oh, yes, their people sent them to America to be away from the War." About the smaller ones I feel rather differently, and in a way, one longs to get them out of it. But there again, one keeps having this strange feeling that Europeans ought to stay in Europe, and take whatever is coming to them, unless, as with you, their homes and families are elsewhere. In any case it is now almost impossible to go. Exit permits are hard to get and they could hardly go by themselves anyway.

Don't worry, we are really all right. We've put the children at Miss H.'s evacuated school in Gloucestershire, which is about as safe as anywhere. They are in a huge grand country house belonging to Lady E. She inhabits half of it, and the school is in the other half. They have superb food, tennis courts, swimming pool, trees to climb, etc. Sir I. spoils them whenever possible. J.'s [the older boy's] school is just being evacuated to Wales. This is great fun, as he'll be fairly near the others. In the holidays we're planning to take a farm-house near Ross-on-Wye, or go as lodgers in one and work on the land, but this, like all our plans, is "subject to the invasion." It is really grotesque to hear people discussing the invasion. One refers to it quite casually as though it was Goodwood or the Eton and Harrow, only, of course, not as certain as either of those.

C—— became impossible—Bren guns along the sand dunes, fixed bayonets in the caddie-shed, barricades along the road, and hellish noise at night. So we removed the children and Nannie (on the day Holland capitulated) and drove westward, ending up at Miss H.'s. Nannie is now with her sister at H——, where her other sister (the army nurse one) is on leave. She was in a mobile ambulance in France, and was all through the retreat to the coast, bombed and machine-gunned for 6 days and nights and with the German tanks only 5 miles behind them all the time. They were bombed right on to the quay at Boulogne. I saw her the next morning, a bit shaky, but not an eyebrow out of place.

Last week was a hell of anxiety. One thought the whole army was inevitably lost, after Leopold's behaviour; in which case, I suppose we'd have been, temporarily at any rate, sunk. But what a miracle of an evacuation! How I wish I'd seen the Fishermen's Armada going out from Dover. I wonder so much if any of our friends among the East Sussex fishermen helped.

One doesn't really know how to write to you about the present situation, because one knows it will have changed so much, for better or worse, by the time you read this letter. Frankly, we're in a jam. But I feel convinced, and so, apparently, do most people, that even if things go badly, even if they land, and have temporary occupation here (which is what Churchill foreshadowed yesterday as a possibility), they will eventually be driven out again. However, this is a remote and gloomy possibility, which one doesn't seriously entertain. The Local Defence Volunteers were a grand idea and give one a great feeling of confidence. One just keeps a weather eye open to suspicious characters along the roads, takes the distributor arm out of one's car at night, and hopes for the best.

As for me, I am leading a nomadic life. T. flung me out of London by main force, saying it worried him to think that we were both there under the same (potential) bombs, because of the children. I didn't want to embark on taking a house till the holidays, if then, so I bought a strong bicycle with a big luggage grid on the back and a sort of butcher boy's rack on front, and I amble about with a small suitcase and a large rucksack, taking the whole thing in the train for long distances. The point of the bike really is that if the railroads get bombed or get jammed up with refugees, I am still mobile, and can get back to the children somehow.

I stayed a few days at H—— with G. F., who has a charming American mother. Then I went to B'ham to the W.'s. They are mostly working on Aircraft production and dropping on their feet from exhaustion trying to replace what was lost in France, and more so. J. W. is just about to be called up, and wants to get into the R.A.F. if possible. Says if one is killed, one is killed outright, and if not it will provide him with some magnificent poems afterwards. Then I came on here, and I am going to Perthshire next week, then back to B'ham again, then to Gloucestershire to the children, then I don't know. . . . (It is all, of course, subject to the INVASION.) It is rather fun in a way going about like this.

T. is very bored, poor darling, about being cooped up in London unable to help with the war except by working at his own job. E. has been called up, Grenadiers. Our darling M. [the maid] had to go back to Ireland, worse luck, as her husband is due to be called up by De Valera. I hope we'll get her back some day.

Oh, well, nobody can say we don't live in an interesting time. As usual on one's birthday, I am in an "auditing" mood; and I wish to state now, that if I am bombed and killed tomorrow I have had a bloody good run for my money. And I think I may claim that the children have been brought up in such a way that they will make very creditable and happy refugees; which is perhaps the highest praise one can offer to any upbringing.

SURREY
July 17, 1940

MY DEAR C.:

I have been meaning to write to you for ages—ever since your most kind cable came—I put off doing so as we were so uncertain as to plans, and so miserable about everything. We almost decided on sending the children

to Jamaica. We were discussing it when your cable came
—then we thought over that for a week and decided Dad-
die might be offended if we sent the children abroad and
not to him. Then neither Nannie nor Miss S. could leave
parents and go with them and I could not bring myself
to leave I. and this country perhaps for years, so after
being very cross and miserable for a few weeks we at last
decided to keep them all here. When the channel ports
fell into enemy hands we sent children to the W.'s, Dorset, as being safer. However when the whole of France
was overrun there was not much object in leaving them
near the coast—away from home, so we have them all
back, and have made an air raid shelter in the cellar. So
far we have been very lucky and only had one warning
but I expect we will all catch it.

NR. CARLISLE
July 24, 1940

MY DEAR C.:

G. and I have been considering this matter very carefully of our coming to America and we have come to
the conclusion that now that we have not got the French
navy to help us, and the Italian submarines are oper-
ating in the Atlantic, and that the Govt. feel compelled
to abandon their scheme, that it is too risky to bring the
children. My dears, we do so appreciate your kind and
most generous invitation, and we shall never forget it,
and it would have been lovely to have seen you.

I came up here at the beginning of July, as M. and the

two younger ones were invited here, and we felt that invasion was so imminent, that I ought to come and bring all the children, as it would be nearer to Liverpool and therefore more possible to get off if we could get a boat to America. As they could not take the two elder children here I remembered Miss B. had two sisters near W——, who took in paying guests, so I let them go there and they are very happy. They are attending the village school and enjoying it very much. Ruth tells me she is using the same Arithmetic book, only the next one more advanced, as she did in her old School. And one wonders why one spends vast sums on one's children's education! Now I have been offered a small house on the Yorkshire border. It is very remote and except for parachutists and such like we should be fairly safe. So M. and I are taking all the family there next week. I feel M. will be well able to cope with a parachutist or two. Further plans one cannot think of; if we are invaded I shall just have to stay put. If we are not—and yet the south does not seem very safe for the children. I shall see if N. will come and take charge and enable me to get back to Cambridge. If O—— seems safer than Cambridge then they will have to go there. Of course really if we can afford it, I should like us all to be back in Cambridge.

Naturally I am longing to get back to G. He is working extremely hard and does really want one there.

Thank you, C., very much for your nice long letter, which I was so glad to get. I can so well understand how you must be feeling. Longing for news of everyone, and mails must take so long. I think quite definitely the "morale" of the country has gone up very much, and our R.A.F. seem really splendid. If we can only get enough planes and be able to attack and attack, that is *the* great thing I am sure, and one does feel the American people are waking up, though I imagine there is a good deal of Nazi propaganda to contend with. Enough of war. It's all nightmarish and I think one of the most trying things is that one just lives from day to day, one cannot make plans or look forward to anything, the future is so dark and uncertain. However, for the children's sake, one must not think of it. They are all so well at present and completely untouched by the war.

HERTFORDSHIRE
July 6, 1940

DEAR C.:

Have been trying for the past fortnight to write to you. And I feel it must appear very surly in us that we have not before thanked you both for your incredibly kind invitation. It's quite unbelievably kind. And we have been almost overcome by the desire of people in America to help. Actually, I very seriously thought of accepting. And bring the children. But after a bad week of indecision, decided that we would all stay together. The uncertainty of the future might have meant leaving D. for years, and we both felt that if the children went I would have to go with them.

One does not want to spare one's children any horror, but the submarine menace might be worse than anything here. There is just the point of view that was expressed in the letters to the *Times* this week; that we don't want the next generation to grow up to feel they can escape anything unpleasant by going away. After all, so far in this country we have been saved for so long from any desperate consequences that I do feel that we've just got to stay and face what comes. And it may not come. Not that Hitler won't try to come, I think that he will have to; but he won't succeed.

Everything is sad and horrible especially the French fleet, but everybody is very calm, and full of determination. There is no defeatism among the village people or anyone. We all know that we are bound to win in the end, but it will be unpleasant while it lasts.

Meanwhile, C., thank you again. It would have been lovely to have seen you all again, and we shall never forget your invitation. It was really very tempting. But the decision is made, and I believe you would have done the same.

HAMPSHIRE
August, 1940

DEAR T.:

Thank you so much for your letter, and for the wonderful offer you and C. have made to us. We want to thank you so very much for such generosity in welcoming us to your home, and we do appreciate what it is to invite a family into your house for an indefinite period and accept responsibility for supporting them. But though we would like to show our appreciation of such friendship by accepting, we both feel quite clear that we want our children to stay in England.

At the moment—though of course we are not in much of a position to judge—it looks as if the war is likely to be long and difficult, but the danger of being killed—or indeed however it goes—seems comparatively slight. X. is, I am very glad, very unlikely, as a civil servant, to be called up for military service. And for the privations, much will remain after the war and it would not be easy for me and the children to enjoy comfort for the duration and then come home to inevitable poverty. And secondly we feel that there will be so much to be learnt in England—even from the privations—for ourselves and for the children too. England is very exciting. I think we are all beginning to think and try and see things clearly and disinterestedly in a new way. If our material standards go down, I think our values are becoming much more real. In a way the only thing I am afraid of is a return to our old life which was so complaisant and involved and content with compromises. I feel I am learning every day just the things that I want most to teach the children and that make it easier and clearer to give them a really Christian home.

So you see we feel that there is very much for us all to gain at home and very little chance of us losing anything important. And indeed, if worse things should happen, which I don't really expect now, we had still rather be here than be refugees, for I am sure that whatever happens if we have enough courage and humility and go on thinking—and no one can deprive you of any of these things—we can make a better society out of the future. And we have no right to deprive our children of their share in that, and how it is made will depend on how we all live now.

V

LONDON AND THE BLITZKRIEG

LONDON AND THE BLITZKRIEG

Letters from women in London; from the days of Dunkirk, through the first August bombings, to the Blitzkrieg.

The "pretty silver cows" referred to here are the barrage balloons of which Londoners are so affectionately proud. They float at varying heights and are moored to trucks. The trucks stand in various open spaces in the London area and are readily movable from place to place. Opinions on their appearance vary: some people compare them to fat fishes, others to baby elephants. Seen from a distance as you approach London, they might be so many tennis balls, surprisingly scattered about in the air. In the day-time they shine silver; at sunrise and sundown, they turn a lovely pastel pink.

LONDON
June 9, 1940

MY DEAR C.:

Our weather has been such a help in these dark days. Using so much less petrol has made the London atmosphere so much clearer and lighter than usual, and the days for the last month have been radiant. We have been back 2 months and are so glad to be home again, and don't intend to leave again unless we are so compelled. We have got things and our household of 3 fairly prepared for air raids! As there have been bombs dropped even on that little place F—— R——, in Sussex, we feel nowhere is really immune, and we outwardly are supported by seeing our pretty "silver cows" in the sky, and our air warden and fire auxiliaries about. The former is no light job nowadays. A nephew and niece of ours (as air wardens) were called up 3 times last night.

M. had his 21st birthday last month and he was promised a week's leave to cover the date and we hoped to have had him, as he has not been home since the end of February. However it was of course all cancelled so we decided to go down to him for 48 hours. He has been on the south coast for the last 3 months with his battery working like a slave and we found him very tired and old-looking. Now he is daily "standing by" before dawn and sleeping in his clothes and ready to move off at an hour's notice—and how fortunate we are to have him on this side! He has been very anxious about 2 friends who we are thankful to hear are amongst the amazing 350,000 saved—what a deliverance.

Our own lives seem so futile, and ineffectual, but at last H. has got several bits of war work on hand. Unless you get into uniform it is extraordinarily difficult to find work (unpaid). So different from the last war. She may go up to the London School of Economics, now evacuated to Cambridge, in the autumn. It is a very hard time to grow up, as I expect you remember—but on thinking it over, I don't think you were grown up in 1914! J. is so well placed with this Hut that really needs doing and which she really can do. She has been hearing wonderful stories from the returned B.E.F.'s who have inundated the Hut. They have taken up to £70 per day, so you can understand the organization and labour that it incurs!

Both D. and I find the daily housekeeping and shopping tiresome, but there is plenty and a great variety of everything except meat which is somehow dull and limited. The crabs have been delicious! I have just heard of an American girl over here who has received a large parcel of groceries from her relations in America, on the supposition that she was in dire need here! Life is expensive, but there is *no want* of food. Our taxation and the 2½ D. postage are a great trial, and it is curious what a difference the latter has made in our letters. We get much fewer, and the telephone is even more popular than it was! S. is well but moves very little and of course is overwhelmed by the ruthless and useless carnage and destruction now going on. It is quite awe-ful. It is worse even than last time. Even the wounds are ghastly. I know how you must feel, being so very far away but I hope you are not amongst isolationists, which must make being away from one's own country so much more difficult. Do you feel really settled in now?

From a member of the family whose letters were given in "Country Dwellers."

The "Book" is a restaurant close by the British Museum, familiar to all who have spent hours in the Museum's reading-room.

LONDON
August, 1940

MY DARLING UNCLE G.:

I've been meaning and waiting to write to you for ages, but somehow life is very hectic and I never get time to settle down. Tonight B. is off learning how to drill with a broomstick so it seems a good opportunity to settle down. Mother says you have offered refuge to the family—if the war lasts long enough I will probably send you my son (or daughter) who should arrive in January. It seems a queer old time to have a baby but in a way it's rather a comfort to have something so utterly one's own to plan for, even if it's only planning ways to get it to safety.

London is much the same as when you left it. Br. and I meet regularly at the "Book" and they still give us delicious lunches. So far it's all very quiet, though some of the Ministries (mine included) have lots of barbed wire entanglements round them and more people carry their gas masks than did in February. We had our first alarm in London last night, so everyone has been a bit bleary eyed today. B. and I dressed, but as we heard no bombs or guns, we stayed where we were, and after a bit I personally curled up on my bed and slept soundly until the all clear woke me. I don't think B. slept so much, in fact I remember waking up for a moment and seeing him poring over a book on higher mathematics. He spends the few moments he isn't working or drilling studying higher mathematics for some terrific exam. he wants to take in the future! He has unbounded energy! I can't compete at all now. I find the 64-hour week now indulged in by the Civil Service, and pregnancy, completely use up my energy. It's not too much, but it's quite enough.

I expect the family will have told you all about M. He seems to have had a terrific time in Flanders and is reputed to have arrived in Brecon in a tin hat, bath towel and a pair of shorts! He lost all his equipment and had to swim out to a boat at Dunkirk. I believe his Brigadier told Dad since that he was really outstandingly efficient and brave. I haven't seen him since he got back, as I couldn't get away when he had leave.

B. and I had a very funny time the other weekend. We managed to get Friday and Saturday off and thought we would go and have a really peaceful few days by the river. We arrived at "a small riverside town" as the Ministry of Information would put it, and went to a little pub where B. had once stayed in the past, right on the river and very attractive. There were a great many soldiers about, but we thought nothing of it, and having found they could give us a room, went off and spent a lovely afternoon in a punt on the river. We got back just in time for dinner, which seemed difficult to procure, and noticed that the dining room was curtained in half. We enquired the reason and found one half was the sergeants' mess of the local unit and that the other half was for guests, who, except for ourselves, appeared to be the sergeants' wives and families. We soon realized that there was no place there for us, so after a walk retired to an early bed. But our hopes of sleep were remote. The wireless was turned full on and the sergeants and their wives held a singsong in competition with it until two in the morning!

"The various wars" refers to the outraged questions put in the House of Commons about the indiscriminate internment of alien refugees. As a result of these questions, many of the "friendly aliens" have been released and conditions have been eased for some of the others.

Tottenham is a suburb in North London, far from any body of water and therefore not a very suitable home for French fishermen.

LONDON
September 2, 1940

I suppose you see *The Times*, so will see all the various wars going on over our unfortunate friends. It really has done some good however and things are being tackled in the right sort of way now. C. has got a family of 5 Belgians living with her. Charming people, the man was a clerk on the railway and they have a daughter of 17 and two nephews aged about 12 and 13. It is really rather a sporting effort and seems to work admirably, especially as she also has an old aunt evacuated on her, also from Belgium.

I saw A. the other day, she is very busy coping with innumerable French refugees, including many families of fishermen, for a time billeted in Tottenham! Can you imagine it! They are gradually getting them fishing permits, but that is not easy just now.

London gets more cosmopolitan every day. You are now liable to meet Poles, Czechs, French, Dutch, Belgian, Norwegian officers and men in all the buses, not to speak of the Dominions. I dined out the other night and on arriving found myself transported to Gibraltar. The two houses on either side had been taken over for Gibraltar and Malta refugees, and the street was literally swarming with little black-eyed children chattering in Spanish, and all the doorsteps were occupied by mothers, old men and babies.

Two letters from a middle-aged professional woman; one written before and one after the Blitzkrieg.

LONDON W.1
July 18, 1940

MY DEAREST C.:

My own news is very nil. I am still working in the House of Lords and of course our hours are erratic; it is difficult to make engagements because I never know what time I will get off, and consequently I see little of my friends. Actually, most people with children have gone into the country, so that, really, the residue of one's acquaintance amounts to very little. London is very calm, and has pulled up its socks to an extent that has greatly altered its appearance! Our little friend, Mr. Hitler, is inaccurate in saying that every private house is a nest of machine-guns, but we have got a tidy lot of emplacements hither and yonder and, at a rough computation, several million miles of barbed wire, plus the nattiest line in air-raid (splinter) shelter for the use of the populace in daylight raids! I had a friend up from the country last weekend and she says the morale in her part of the world, where they are having practically nightly raids, is excellent; everyone realizes that we are bound to be in for a very bad time, but it was an immense relief to the public generally to hear Winston's speech the other night and to know that the Cabinet is going to be strong enough to see us suffer—a difficult thing for men who are responsible for the well-being of the people, but that was where the weakness of the French Government came in. It is not the French people who have given in; they were sold by weaklings.

But I am sure our strongest weapon is faith and prayer. Did they reproduce in U. S. A. that letter from an Airman to his mother? It was exactly the spirit of England and put one's own feeling so well.

Yes, I know the *Song Celestial* well. It has been my constant companion for at least twelve years and is a perpetual joy. I have given copies to several of my young

friends lately and they find it the same help and en-
lightenment that we do. I haven't got the Mystical Col-
lects book. I had forgotten about it, but I will get it out
of the Theosophical Library some time. Mostly I have
been rereading old friends such as *The Growth of the
Soul*, *Tertium Organum*, etc., but work, knitting and
correspondence do not leave many cracks for intensive
study.

I have blossomed into knitting socks and am filled
with sinful pride when I view their symmetry and beauty!
I am as proud as a dog with two tails as I am not one
of those fortunate wights who are clever with their hands,
and consequently even so pedestrian an achievement as
a pair of socks fills me with self-satisfaction out of all
proportion!

Food is likely to become more difficult with France's
defection, and having to evacuate the Channel Islands,
but so far we have had absolutely no shortage at all and
cannot in the least complain. Not that we could complain anyhow; we have just got to get down to things
if this evil is to be rolled back and destroyed. I agree
with all you say about it being a battle between good
and evil. As long ago as four years back a friend of mine
who had been working in Germany, Austria and Czecho-
Slovakia said to me when she came back that, whilst she
didn't wish to sound imaginative (she is actually a very
practical non-mystical woman) or hysterical, she must
say to me that all the time she was in Germany she had
an almost concrete sense of evil being abroad. And I

think it was and is. They have harboured evil, and nourished evil, and evil will destroy them from within.

My sister has had three H.E. bombs in the field in which she exercises the [word omitted, probably horses] and six more in a neighbouring field, and several incendiary bombs, but the village wasn't touched, and the total damage but five cows killed. (N.B. My cousin's maid refers to them as "insanitary bombs" and feels much more comfortable in her mind now that she has bought "A really good fire distinguisher, miss!!!") I don't suppose the invasion and intensive air warfare can be long delayed, but I have sent my drawing room curtains to be cleaned this morning, feeling that I really cannot have my domestic arrangements upset by the mere Hun!

LONDON W.1
October 7, 1940

MY DEAREST C.:

Your two letters arrived last week. I was so glad to have them and to know that my own epistle had reached you. One casts one's bread upon the waters in a spirit of hope, and trusts to a kindly Providence to guide it to its destination, but so frequently nowadays letters vanish into space—doubtless due to some indiscretion of one's own!

I went to S—— Place on Saturday afternoon which was the first opportunity I had of doing so. G. is still there and does not know when he will be called up; it is so much a matter of having room for the men, with such a large number under arms, and all training camps now concentrated in the British Isles. Before, we expected to do that work in France. We went up to the flat and I had a general look around. The upholstered furniture is covered in its holland covers and dustsheets, and is of course all right, but naturally the rest of the flat is very dusty. Would you like me to send my maid down once a fortnight to Hoover it and just keep the dust from settling into carpets and curtains? We could cover the wood furniture with newspaper and if the curtains were given an occasional Hoovering, it would keep them from deteriorating. The books in the cases are of course quite snug. Your windows are, I am thankful to say, so far intact. The Hamilton Place bomb (which shattered every window in Londonderry House) only broke one of your building's panes.

I am lucky so far, as although my area has been absolutely plastered, and I can see five craters and heaps of what were once houses in a straight line from my bedroom window and we have had a bomb 50 yards down the mews behind us (two blocks of those flats which run at right angles to my block are down and two more of the same Mansions are down just a little bit further away from me), none of our windows have gone. The house across the entry at my end of the block was burnt out by incendiaries, but again we were lucky and the fire didn't reach us. You just can't imagine the pluck and courage of the Firemen and the A.R.P. wardens.

You have got to remember they have to do their work in the dark, except for the glare of the fires, and you have no idea till you see them at it, how difficult it is locating hydrants, etc., without proper light. And once the fires get going Fritz briskly seizes the opportunity to drop more bombs, so that a number of firemen have been killed in that way, and it has added much to the difficulties and danger.

But they all carry on quite unperturbed and at our fire, once they had ascertained that there was no one in the building, and that we, in ours, were ready to evacuate at once if necessary, they were laughing and cracking jokes quite regardless of the fact that the roof was in imminent danger of giving way beneath them, and that incendiaries were still dropping.

We had a busy evening haring about with buckets of sand; incendiaries are quite easy to put out if you keep your head and get them in time. The trouble is when they fall through a roof without being seen and get a grip before being dealt with; that is what happened at Day, Son's and Hewett's. They dropped in on the mews side so of course we never saw them.

As regards the actual bombing, of course there has been a great deal of damage done in London, but not nearly so much as you would expect considering the effort Fritz has expended, and of course it is all to the good that it should be civilian damage and not military or industrial. We all feel that. Taken all round, they have achieved very little, and people are absolutely set-

tling down to it, and taking the raids in their stride. During the day no one pays the slightest attention to them.
We go on working here (in the House of Lords) with
guns all around and machine guns overhead; I presume
if bombs actually dropped round us the whistle *would*
go and the survivors would repair to the shelters (!!!)
but to date the Fighter Command's idea of "Danger
Imminent" does not seem likely to include gunfire and
planes overhead. It has become a joke with us now; we
say it is like the grocer's grading of eggs—"Fresh," "New
Laid" and "Today's."

At night I do now sleep in the basement, as the vi-
bration from our barrage is so terrific that I shouldn't
close an eye upstairs. Also, though it is all really a matter of chance where the bomb lights, on the whole I
think the survival value of a basement is slightly higher!
The courage of the "common man" is really superb.
They take most things with a laugh, and in the evenings,
before settling down for the night, my maid and her
husband (whom I have brought to live in the flat as
their house was in a very dangerous area, being between
a railway terminus and a power station) play cards with
the porter and his wife in the latter's sitting room, and
their bursts of laughter come floating out to me as I read
in the hall, against a background of barrage and bombs!
And it is genuine enjoyment too. Sometimes it is so in-
fectious that I find myself smiling just to hear them.
And the people in the streets, going off to the shelters
with their mattresses, are always ready to laugh as they

pass you, and crack a joke. And if an unexploded Delayed Action bomb goes off as you are walking along,
passers-by usually grin at each other and remark, "There
goes another." Nobody hurries though.

You would feel, as I do, very proud of your fellow-
countrymen and women if you were amongst them and
saw the quite unself-conscious everyday manner in which
they take everything, and how well they behave even
with H.E. dropping like leaves in Vallombrosa. They are
just GRAND.

I am very fortunate that the raids don't seem to affect me; even the bomb in the mews, which I really did
think was the end as it came down, left me quite unmoved. And I sleep very well indeed, now that I am
used to a mattress on the floor. I don't pray for protec-
tion or for life, because I realize that whatever comes is
what I myself have engendered in past lives, but I do
ask, if continued life is granted me, that I may be helped
to use that life to the service of God, and, if death or
maiming is my portion, that I may be given strength
and fortitude, by grace, to accept what comes. And having done that each night, I think no more about it.

It is difficult to know what to say about coming back;
I honestly don't know what you would do in London;
I don't think you are strong enough to do war work,
and it is practically impossible to see much of friends;
also the authorities very rightly don't want any more
people in dangerous areas than have to be there. And
your flat is very high and has got a lot of glass. It is the

glass which really makes me go downstairs; having seen the incredible things that blast can do with glass, I feel grimly that it is to the general interest as well as to my own, to keep out of the way of it as much as possible. We are still shaking glass out of our shut files, as a result of our bomb *outside* this building last week. And one staircase is just a yawning chasm; nothing left but a little frill of stone running up the sides of the wall—all due to blast. However, you must decide on such a matter yourself.

Have just finished John Buchan's *Memory Hold the Door* and loved it; his prose has a Biblical quality of balanced rhythm that is very satisfying to my Presbyterian ear. He has some lovely phrases.

One of my cousins is doing work in one of the suburbs and on Friday a German plane, flying so low they thought it would foul the chimneys, machine-gunned children on their way home from school. She says they could actually see the pilot so he *must* have known it was children. And anyhow deliberately to machine gun civilians is quite unspeakable.

From a private secretary in a publishing office.

CENTRAL LONDON
September 4, 1940

DEAR S. AND N.:

I had a week's holiday during the first week of the blitzkrieg, and my son was suddenly granted seven days' leave. His latest girl friend was free too, so we hired a car for the week, and were allowed enough petrol to go 400 miles! So we eked it out, getting as far as the Hog's Back one day and Box Hill another, etc. Then we parked the car and went hiking. It was lovely for F. to be in a sports outfit, including sandals.

C. B. refuses to change his mode of life one iota. If the sirens go, and he's in his bath he carries on, and proceeds on his way to the office, raid or no raid. Actually, we've had a lot of warnings, but that's all. S. says we must go to our office shelter, in spite of the inconvenience, and H. concurs for he nearly stopped a couple of bombs when he was taking a walk last Sunday. The night warnings are a bit of a nuisance, but I always go to sleep and rarely hear the "all-clear." I think a lot of people do the same. After all, it would be much nicer to be asleep if something is going to hit you—but actually the damage done is far less than one expects. There are lots of shelters now—quite respectable brick-built ones—besides guns, bayonets and barbed wire here and there. However, we seem to have settled down. It's funny to see the horses being removed from their shafts in Covent Garden, and then seeing the men staring heaven-wards (not that there is anything to see) instead of taking cover.

J. is in the Air Force in an advisory capacity, or something. Anyway, it is non-combatant. He's thrilled at the nerve of the airmen. One bailed out, and while coming down made a tourniquet below his knee with the aid of his fountain pen (his foot had been shot away) and so saved his life—to fly again.

We're getting plenty to eat. In fact, plenty of everything—and are ready for any drastic rationing. We're being careful about buying new clothes. My sister has given me a winter coat, so that I can put the money in the war doings instead.

LONDON N. 7
September 19, 1940

MY DEAR G.:

I am having to write to your old address, the only one I know now, and hope that the letter reaches you.

You will be sorry to hear that D. and I are homeless, and have only what we stand in owing to having a direct hit by an H.E. in the garden.

I was downstairs talking to the landlady when the bomb fell, and I never want to experience again what I experienced last Sunday week the 8th. I saw the furniture in her sitting room rise, and the back half of her house collapse. We were buried in the debris. How ever I got her out of it I do not know. We were both pretty badly shaken, and it's not too pleasant to get a good whiff of coal gas. My nerves are not too good either after that lot and I just dread the air raids now, and I wish that I was miles from London.

I don't know what is going to happen as our house is completely wrecked and it is not too easy to get clothes either these days. We are both temporarily put up in a school, and it is not too comfortable or pleasant.

When you write put same address on envelope (House wrecked will call at sorting office) as I have to call at sorting office for letters.

Where is this all going to end, G.? The damage in London is dreadful. Poor old A., he is upset about it. We have had a pretty tough blow.

From an ex-governess, now married, to a woman who was a pupil of hers for 10 years and who is now an evacuated mother in the U. S. A.

WIMBLEDON, LONDON
October 23, 1940

MY DEAREST J.:

Oh, how pleased I was to get your letter and all the exciting news. You can't think how stirring some jolly old news is—thrills at the moment seem at a premium!

Time bomb just gone off, half the roads around us seem "No Entry" ones, patiently waiting for these fiends to explode! I am glad you like the U. S. A. and people, it must be a marvellous change to get right away into new environment, even if life is hectic as it sounds. I was really thankful you got away, as we have had a fairly hectic time, but, my dear, people are amazing, all so plucky, whatever the odds, and my heavens, it must be an uncomfortable time for heaps of them.

[292]

The cheery way some woman said to me the other day, "Never mind, we have escaped with our lives," surrounded by the most utter mess imaginable.

Of course one luckily gets accustomed to a lot of it, the barrage doesn't bother me at all, the whine of the bombs is the most disconcerting, however even that passes quickly, and one is rather thrilled after every escape.

We have our shelter delightfully cosy now. We had to spend a lot on it to get it drained, but have duck boards, ground sheets, mattress and eiderdown on floor and bunks either side, portable wireless and electric light.

However we just had to give it some appeal, as we retire down there about 7 until 6 A.M. or so.

Before we could sleep there we had wretched nights and were so tired, but we are heaps better now and sleep, on the whole, fairly well. I feel sleep and meals are the two chief concerns to keep one going and one grows more like a bunny rabbit every day.

Sirens going now but we go down only if they are overhead and the guns firing. Some days the raids amount to very little but warnings, whereas other days you get little peace—often 6 or 7 warnings a day and much noise.

But people walk about much more, and business just has to go on, as it wastes so much time hanging around.

S.'s office got badly blasted by a bomb which demolished a place opposite to him. You never saw such a mess and all round him. I went up one day to see it all. So now he is working at home, which is much nicer for me. He just goes up on Mondays only.

Of course there has been colossal damage to houses and business premises, but the military targets they fail to hit, which is lucky. They are always after the lines too.

M. writes that they had 200 bombs dropped near her, terrifying but not a single casualty. D—— poor marksmanship!! What a marvellous escape for everybody and everything!

All clear now, so very short affair, but the weather, we rejoice to see, is damp and foggy at last. We had our most peaceful night last night.

It has been such a glorious autumn, if only we had been allowed to enjoy it more. One blessing—one year of this curse has gone. Human endurance is quite surprising, no limits to it. Of course fear and anticipation are the most devastating. Once you have to face up to it all, it rather astonishes even yourself, how you go through.

I've never been away since May, and I don't go out much, however the days just fly, one seems always busy.— I think this retiring so early takes up so much time. We have to feed at 6, change and skedaddle down at 7. But we have had the electric light only a few days, so we can do more now. Previously we had just a wee oil lamp, which was all right for a short time, but with the darkness we had to have more light.

I feel we are so lucky to have our own shelter, when

you realize all the crowds huddled together in tubes and public shelters. I find so many of your bits are so useful and cosy for nights, including the orange cloak and your old squirrel coat.

From an A.R.P. worker.

AIR RAID POST IN LONDON W. 1
September 16, 1940

DEAR N.:

Take my advice and keep away from the headlines for a bit. Letters will tell you much more accurately how the war is getting on.

The thing to hang on to is that London is vast and that they don't bomb everywhere all the time. I was most surprised about this. A bit naïve about bombings, I thought the sky would be black with bombers 24 life-times a day, if you see what I mean.

But it isn't a bit like that.

We're getting used to being a nation of buttons on bits of elastic with the sirens holding the other end and tweaking us underground.

As a matter of fact, I do A.R.P. telephones and that means that every other night from midnight to sixish, I phone for fire squads and report incidents and (thank God) make tea, and every other night S. does it. And every day I report during Sirens (there's one on now) but most times I stay in my flat, which is just along

the corridor from the post, and only go when needed—
as now.

So I'm lucky because once at the post I think of
bombs as "Incidents" and not as what they are doing
to London, and that makes it much better. We had a
large "incident" the other day—or rather night—and the
building rocked and the emergency lights went out, and
when it settled back again, I emerged from under the
telephone table and said, "Local Bomb makes good"—
and not a soul laughed. Still I didn't have much time
to sulk on account of three fires to send other people
out to cope with.

But again, London is vast and—sans blague—glorious,
and the people are the salt of the earth. We only stop
quarrelling at our post when things are hailing down.
We are composed of blimps and ex-soldiers and coun-
ter-attendants and one elderly female.

And we've got a very fine barrage now and I can't
tell you the difference it has made us feel about raids.
I never thought I should look on gun fire as a lullaby,
but I do and so do other people.

S. and I have got a tin hat between us. S. looks vaguely
Japanese in it and I look definitely orphaned.

Of course it's terrible for people who have to go down
to shelters with children, all night long.

We're furious with the foe over Buckingham Palace.
Clearly he is nothing but a hooligan. He'll be writing
rude messages in the sky any time now.

Well, the gun fire is getting a bit heavy so I'll adopt a slightly—ever so slightly—more alert attitude.

P.S. A bit about clothes and fun and theatres, please. Ours have closed down for a bit. Still they'll come bobbing up again soon, I guess. The worst thing to be brave about is the tea ration. Everything else can be managed.

Two letters from a London Ambulance Driver, written during a well-earned rest in the country.

SHROPSHIRE
October 11, 1940

DEAREST J.:

I am enjoying a much-needed rest. It is quite wonderful to have quiet nights and days of utter leisure. But I go back tomorrow evening, and as E. remarks, I expect I shall mind going back to it all much more than I think. I got quite used to it lately and became what I would have thought early in September quite brave.

The country is at its best. Lovely clear fresh autumn days and all the trees rich in yellows and browns and distant blues and the ground is covered with coloured leaves on top of wet earth. Here you can see no sign of the war except in the sky. Training planes boom overhead all day. This morning we made bonfires for getting rid of the dead wood: flames and billowing smoke through the sunlight and shadows of the woods and the crackle of burning leaves and sticks. How lovely England is.

I want to know some more about America, especially the country places. How I long to go there and if there is a penny left after the war I should love to make the trip. But I expect you will want to come back. In between the bouts of thinking of the horrors of war and the horrors of the final outcome and what will happen to us all, whether in defeat or victory, I manage to feel fairly happy. I don't seem to see any of the same people that I used to before the London bombing started. I seem to be thrown into a new world—mostly the station, they are the easiest to see.

If you were to come to your beloved London now you wouldn't at first notice very much change. There is a great deal of exaggeration. But when you look down side streets you are apt to see a heap of rubble in the road and a gap in the row of houses. There was a bomb on St. Mary's, but it hasn't even broken the windows of your house.

I have had, lately, to be more or less in charge of my shift at the Ambulance station. A terrifying job, sitting by the telephone, waiting for a call and ordering people about much older than myself and ticking people off for things I did myself a week before. Our commandant has been told by the L.C.C. to report any cases of fortitude or endurance, so of course we are all hoping to get the George Medal. You put G.M. after your name like D.S.O.

Sherry has just come in—the room is very quiet. D. and S. are reading. I can only hear a crackly fire. It's a delicious autumn evening in the country after a day out of doors. Now I look forward to a pre-dinner bath and then wearing my ancient evening clothes—all this in the manner of before the war, and we have talked very little of it today. At these moments of great peacefulness, I always feel faintly sad.

LONDON

November 21, 1940

DARLING J.:

Well, on goes the bombing. London is beginning to show her scars, and there are some heartrending sights. I think St. James's, Piccadilly, moved me more than anything. It stands, but the top of the tower has gone, there is no roof. The beautiful windows are buckled up and broken. The courtyard is full of débris. The gateway is crooked and dangerous and it will never be the same again whatever people say about building a replica. Opposite, the fifty-shilling tailor is a heap of wood, concrete and rusty iron, but clearly matters less. John Lewis's is a vast heap of devastation—a few iron girders crawling into the sky, ruined pillars overturned and the lettering and draperies falling down, crooked and hanging and dusty.

A land mine exploded on [cut out by censor] destroying it utterly—that dignified late Georgian building—but I haven't seen it. Not long ago, one of the biggest

[299]

explosives known dropped [censored] from my house. We were sitting at the top in my room and heard the inevitable whistle and then, for what seemed ages after the explosion, the sound of falling masonry. Our house shook like a leaf and crackled as though it was made of paper. I knew then what it would feel like if it really was going to fall and carry us with it. Nine houses were totally demolished and seventeen made uninhabitable— roofs blown off, etc. The crater [censored] and there were at least twenty people killed—mostly buried under the rubble. The rescue squads were days digging them out. Immediately afterwards a time bomb fell on [censored] so after a large amount of alcohol consumed in the pub under heavy gunfire I evacuated for a week. It was an intolerable nuisance but we are back now, thank God.

About a week later, another good sized bomb fell on top of [censored] station. A train was there at the time and there were about fifty dead—not only dead but mutilated beyond all recognition. Most of the digging consisted of getting out arms, legs, etc., separately and packing them up in labelled bundles to be sent to the mortuary to be sorted out. Our ambulances were out all that night (and next day with reliefs). I didn't go because I had to be at the telephone sending them out one after another. An inglorious work and deadly.

There is no doubt the Germans are pretty hard at it and I can't think why they don't send more. But perhaps they prefer the slow agony of pure chance hits.

London has settled down to it. I take no more notice at all and never dream of going to a shelter or any longer sleeping anywhere but in my own bed. If I am bombed—all right, but until then I shall be comfortable and as little tired as possible. Several people at the ambulance station have had bombs on their houses but have escaped in various ways. One man had everything he possessed destroyed, and, when commiserated with, said, "After all, we are both young and strong and can set up a home again. When one door shuts, another always opens." Later he was seen carrying a small suitcase and held it up saying, "I'm just taking my house away."

Jokes are made daily and it is still the main social topic of conversation. The result of it all is that it is very difficult to know where anyone is living—very difficult to see people. Everyone has a stoic cheerfulness and there is a great deal of heartbreaking bravery and moving incidents. The raids have become part of life. I have just overheard the following: A. "There's a raid on, isn't there?" B. "No, there isn't." C. "Yes, of course there is." B. "Oh. We don't see much of so-and-so these days, do we?" A. "Well, she's got a new job, you know," etc. Evenings are so much changed. No cinemas, theatres or gaiety of any kind and only people scurrying home, tin hats bobbing past one in the streets and a few A.R.P. cars whizzing by on deserted streets.

People study the weather: "Good night for bombing." "Lovely night, isn't it?" "Yes, I wish it wasn't." "Isn't this rain filthy in the blackout—the bombs don't seem to mind, do they?" etc. Pubs are full all the time. Here at the station we are keeping going fairly well. I have become an expert at Pingpong. Next week we are to have a tournament—knockout handicap.

We all become more and more separated and out of touch. That I can't bear. One forgets people and they forget one too. But I have got some new friends here.

My health is absolutely bounding except for exhaustion at times. Sometimes I feel very excited, perhaps just because of the times we live in. The National Gallery [concerts] continue in the basement. I play the gramophone more than ever and music means increasingly more to me—so does poetry, but I seldom read it, or read at all. But I am not superficially depressed, only when I think hard, but that applies to everyone.

Some firemen have just arrived but no one seems to know where it is, so that's off. Now I must stop.

From a young surgeon's wife, trained in nursing and now a hospital organizer.

LONDON W. 1.
October 10, 1940

MY DEAR D.:

I heard a few days ago that Prue had arrived safely in New York. I should be awfully grateful if you would look her up occasionally. I have had no letter from A. since her original cable offering to have Prue. I think it is wonderful of you and F. to do so much for your English friends. I had a most delightful letter from Mrs. C. offering to have Prue. You had apparently passed my letter on before A. decided to have her. She sent me snaps of themselves and their children and I was very touched at total strangers writing and offering Prue a home like that. I don't suppose you can realize what it means to us over here, at a time like this, to feel that our children are safe and well cared for in your country. As I write, there is the usual nightly bombardment going on. I am so used to it that I pay no more attention to it than to a bad thunderstorm. It is only when one hears the whistle through the air of bombs falling close at hand that one pays any attention.

In my own case, I put my fingers in my ears till after the subsequent crash and then go on with whatever I was doing at the moment. I am awfully glad that I have a flat on the first floor here; it means I can go to bed at night in the usual way, feeling comparatively safe, plugging ears and go to sleep. People on the upper floors bring mattresses down on to the lower landings and the basement and sleep there. They stake their claims quite early in the day to be sure of a good place! It's awfully funny really, coming in late in the evening sometimes, to have to step over recumbent forms in various stages of undress all over the corridors!

D. is in Belfast having a very good time, I believe. I am rather tempted to go and join him, as everything is peaceful there, but I should feel I was running away if

I did. I may change my mind when the winter evenings come and the nonsense starts about 5 P.M.!

I wonder if the time will come when we shall all be leading normal lives again and going to parties, etc. If one goes out to dinner nowadays in London it is an understood thing that one stays the night—it's the only way. On the first night of the Blitzkrieg, I dined with M. at her friends' in Grosvenor Square and finally insisted on going home at 1.30, thinking I should pick up a taxi. The long and short of it was, I had to walk all the way, and it was pretty awful, I don't mind telling you, especially as it was only the beginning and one hadn't got one's eye in! There was a terrific fire down in the docks which lit the whole sky with a lurid red glow and the streets were as light as day, but a horrid uncanny light. It was a positive nightmare. . . .

I've just had to stop and put my fingers in my ears, but it wasn't this street, thank goodness!!

Three letters from an unmarried lady who works on a Soldiers' Comforts Committee.

KENSINGTON, LONDON
September, 1940

DARLING G.:

Last Monday—I was with T.—their Electricity plant got it and we had no electricity all day. It was awful with no wireless and not even able to make a cup of

[304]

tea. I have a good little "Meta" cooker here so E. fetched it.

The warning went a few minutes ago and as I now hear the A.A. guns, I must leave this for a while and get away from the windows. This is the third time so far today, but as a rule, the day-time raids do not last very long. It is these nasty seven or eight-hour night-time ones which are so trying. Aren't we proud of our R.A.F.! Fancy bringing down 185 enemy planes yesterday! Fancy the wretches going for Buckingham Palace like they have done. The guns are quiet so I will go on for a little longer. We are getting used to doing our jobs in spurts and just carry on unless the gun fire sounds near. The beginning of the week we felt so helpless hearing these enemy planes over all the time, but now our A.A. are putting up such a good defence we feel much happier.

KENSINGTON, LONDON
September 2, 1940

MY DEAREST G.:

After a quiet and undisturbed night, I feel just right for a chat with you. What a week we have had with air-raid warnings every day, but you would be surprised to see how calmly we go on with our doings, and Herr Hitler will find out his mistake if he thinks he can break down our morale in this way. Our Air Force is just wonderful and over 1,000 planes for the month of August must be giving him something to think about!

[305]

We have had raids every day, and one day—I think it was Thursday—we had seven. Fortunately in the daytime they are soon driven off and we get a fairly big bag, but the night ones are more worrying. One lasted from 11 P.M. till nearly dawn. I went to bed about midnight but at 2 A.M. our big guns were so noisy and the explosions sounded rather too near to be pleasant, so I partly dressed and went down to the second floor and joined a party of friends in the corridor and stayed there until 3.30. Then, as it was much quieter, I came back to bed and stayed there and the "All Clear" went soon after 4 o'clock.

I feel much safer now that I have moved my bed into the corner of the room, well away from both windows, and unless the gunfire is intense I shall stay there, though it is nice to know that there is always my little corner kept for me downstairs if I get lonely.

We only had one yesterday at 2 o'clock just as I was ready to go to friends in Chelsea. It only lasted half an hour so we were not very late. From that time we have been free until 8 o'clock this morning when we had a short one. One can only make "provisional" dates these days, but there is one thing, everybody knows why one is held up and one can only wait until the "All Clear" sounds, for I, for one, will not go out during the raid. The buses carry on and some people walk about, but it is no use tempting Providence if it is not necessary.

You say you wonder whether we know how anxious Americans are to help, and how much they are doing.

Yes, I think we do and we think it is just wonderful
how much you all are doing for the Red Cross, etc. A
Mrs. U. who lives in this building, is quite busy at our
Red Cross Head Quarters and she was telling me of
the huge quantities of partly worn and even new clothing which is coming from New York for the refugees.
She helped to sort them and she says they really are
wonderful, and some are individual parcels beautifully
packed, often containing little extras such as packets of
chocolate, cigarettes, etc., done up in socks, etc. These
things are appreciated very much I know. Every week
more and more planes and supplies are coming to us,
and this will make all the difference when we do the
attacking. We have not the number of planes the Germans have but we are losing very few pilots as against
the hundreds which they will find it difficult to replace.
Anyhow, we are a year nearer VICTORY than we were at
this time last year.

KENSINGTON, LONDON
October 20, 1940

MY DARLING G.:

I am afraid this will not be a very long letter as I have
had a rather busy day and am very tired. However as I
am leaving in the morning soon aften ten o'clock, I
must get a few lines written to you tonight if the devils
overhead will leave us in peace a little while. We have
had six warnings during the day and they have started
their evening visit and it is not 8 o'clock yet. We have

had rather a bad week of it and last night, or rather this morning, several incendiary bombs were dropped around here. Two landed on the roof, two inside of our court-yards and one or two just outside the building. It was about a quarter past one and I had just put out the light and was hoping to get to sleep when there was an awful noise very near. I covered my head up with the bed-clothes and waited for the worst to happen, but for-tunately it didn't, so in a few moments the other Miss W. and I went out into the corridor and joined several other tenants. Almost at once, two A.R.P. wardens rushed up the staircase, but before they reached the roof, two of the tenants had put out the fires with the stirrup pump. They didn't do any damage as we fortunately have a concrete roof, and the others outside were soon ex-tinguished.

The planes and our guns were very busy all night, but we were left in peace and we were very glad it was incendiary and not "land" bombs which got us.

Last Tuesday we had a shock too. I was reading in my bed when, about the same time, 1 o'clock, we had a frightful thud and I was certain the roof had been hit. My bed rocked and I really thought the walls would cave in. But we heard afterwards that it was a land mine which demolished several houses in a street higher up Church Street. All the doors of wardrobes, cupboards, etc., which were not locked, burst open, the pictures and mirrors swung on their chains, and in the sitting room several ornaments had fallen and were rolling about the floor. It reminded me of being aboard ship, but somehow this is more frightening. I feel that this is a very strongly built building to stand up against all this. I suppose, being on a hill, they must make the foundations pretty strong. I wonder when they will find a way to stop this wanton destruction. . . .

Well, I expect, before this you will be wondering where I am going tomorrow. I will tell you all about it. Yesterday quite early—no, I mean the day before, Friday—L. W. phoned to ask if I would not pay them a little visit and have at least a few peaceful nights. I shall enjoy a rest from this continuous noise, and it will be nice to be able to undress fully and go to bed.

When I come back, Miss W. and I are going to sleep in a vacant flat on the second floor as everyone says we are too high up on the fifth floor. We have both bought a small bed which we can drag out into the corridor if we feel there are too many windows in the flat. Personally I feel safer in my own bedroom now I have put the bed in the corner and so missing all the windows, but it might be a question of getting us out if the top floors collapsed.

When I return it will be almost time for T. and E. to go to Bournemouth. I am glad they are going but I hate the idea of being all alone in London, I mean without anybody belonging to me. These are the times when one wants one's family with one. Don't worry about me for perhaps I shall decide to leave too. Now the fear of invasion seems to be past, for the present at least, I might decide to go to M. for a few days and look around Bournemouth, to see if I can find a reasonable hotel where I could stay for a time. I don't want to have this extra expense, but anyhow we won't have any money left when this dreadful war has been paid for, so I might as well pay for a little safety now.

I had a letter from L. yesterday. I don't know whether I told you that, when they bought this smaller house in Buckinghamshire, they stored the greater part of their furniture from their large Hampstead one. Well, the depository where they stored it has been bombed and burnt out, and they have lost everything. They may get some compensation after the war, but, as L. says, there were so many things which had a sentimental value.

Now, my dearest, if you will forgive a rather short letter, I will finish as I really am rather tired and had better do a little packing while there is a quiet interval. A few minutes ago I heard bombs explode somewhere near enough to make the walls vibrate so I brought the typewriter away from the window. It is no use stopping for the devils. We just carry on with what we are doing and hope for the best.

My very best love and please give some to all my nice friends. How I wish I were with you all this very minute. Don't worry. Everything is O.K.

Two letters from the seventy-year-old widow of a General.

The "old man who sells papers at Hyde Park Corner,"

*referred to in the second of these letters, has been there
for many years. He is really a pavement artist, not a newspaper seller, though he sits on the pavement very near
the newspaper kiosk. He always has a topical witticism
chalked up on a blackboard beside him. Hyde Park Corner is the entrance to central London—where Knightsbridge (leading to Kensington and the western district)
joins Piccadilly, by the gates of Hyde Park. That is where
St. George's Hospital is, and the Iron Duke's House.
Buckingham Palace is only a short distance away.*

KENSINGTON, LONDON
September 6, 1940

MY DEAR M.:

We are very busy over the "Battle of London." Our
men are simply splendid, so is everybody. Raid going on
now, so I will have plenty of time to write you a long
letter as one can't go out and they generally last hours.
I began at first jotting down how many we had in a
day, but when it came to 7 in under 24 hours the job
became boring; last night was a particularly long one,
9:15 P.M. to 4:45 A.M. and then a little fun from 5:15
A.M. to 5:45 A.M., but all that you can read in the papers.
The first time or so, I spent hours in the cellar, but it is
really boring, and so hot and smelly, I never go down
there now; a seat on the ground floor, if the noise becomes loud, but I prefer to stay in bed and read a book.

There is an old man who sells papers at Hyde Park

[311]

Corner who regularly chalks up funny remarks. I rather liked today's, "Yes, Bill, Nazi planes are made in Germany and finished in England." Also the story about the village folk who went blackberrying. There were bombs dropped all around them and a little machine-gunning, so they all slipped into a ditch and crept under the hedges, and all they said to each other when it was over, "Look now, Susan, at my nice berries, all covered with dirt, drat them Germans." I admire the ingenuity of the person who advised growing mustard and cress over the Thames, so as to camouflage the river.

A friend of mine had a narrow escape the other day; she went down to shut up her house near the sea, stayed there 4 nights, on the fifth night a bomb through the roof and very little house left, I fear.

Please thank America, the United States, for the magnificent gifts arriving incessantly. I work in Belgrave Square, French Red Cross. The other day when I arrived there were 5 huge cases from U. S. A. on the pavement, we could not shift them till some sailors came along and they carried them up to our floor. We have soldiers and sailors, civilians and all sorts of odds and ends. They come with a *"bon"* on which is written what they are to have, and sometimes when one is not too hurried there is time to listen to their often tragic stories. They are all joining de Gaulle's forces, or civilians get work in war factories. About 3 weeks ago letters were again accepted for *unoccupied* France, but the post takes weeks even if it arrives at all. Imagine the agony of these

poor folk, no news of their families, who are for the
most part in occupied France and they themselves considered as traitors to be shot by the foul Vichy Government; also many of them cannot get work at once, knowing no English, can't read papers or understand the wireless, no money, no work. Last week a French paper was
started for them, which must be a great comfort to de
Gaulle's people.

We now have 2 fine-looking French policemen to help
us as the running up and down stairs does one in. I only
go in the afternoons, cannot manage all day, too exhausting. I had a fine old Boulogne fisherman to "dress" the
other day, his cottage destroyed, he escaped in his fishing
boat and brought 17 people, 2 old dames of 80 and a
baby of 7 months. There was a very funny man from
Dunkerque, very fat, and most queer body, a fisherman
with a very fat little round stomach, and he could not
make up his mind where to wear his leather belt, above
or below; I found him a very outsize pullover and some
brown boots, he said he had never worn *brown* boots
before, but I told him it was very smart, and with a very
gaudy tie and a hat much too small for him, he stepped
about the room saying, "Voici le chic Anglais." He could
coin money on the Music Hall Stage. The sailors and
soldiers that come are always most charming men, especially the sailors, and very clever at tying up their own
parcels, in fact won't let one do it; civilians generally
look on, sometimes too shy perhaps to offer to help.

So far, I have been very lucky and never been caught

in the streets in a very long raid. There is a most elegant shelter at 27 Knightsbridge by Heath the Hatter. There are arm chairs, electric light, very clean and does not smell, and every convenience. I have been there 3 times. The Underground and Tube Stations shut immediately and busses stop, mostly, and you have to get out and go to a shelter. You can generally get a taxi, I did the other day as it was just lunch time, I had no food on me and did not fancy having to wait perhaps for hours, though I need not have fussed as all clear went in three-quarters of an hour, but one never knows. I have given up going out in the evening, it would be so awful to be caught in a public shelter for hours, and after all one is quite comfortable in one's own hotel.

Think you will get tired of reading all this, so I will now stop. I hear no guns, but all clear has not gone yet, so I suppose they are still about. The weather is very hot, and one has to black out now at 8 P.M., but you can leave your window open if there is no wind to disarrange the black blind and curtains. The streets look like a perpetual Bank Holiday, but busses rush at a fine pace as there are no blocks. At night busses look like queer kinds of ships, they have dimmed lights inside, but you don't exactly see the lower part of them, so it makes them look very strange in the distance. The A.R.P. have a tough time making folk go into shelters in a raid as people, especially the working classes, have a mania of standing on the doorsteps and gaping at the sky in case they may see a good fight.

All the same, how one wishes it was all over and how bitterly one grieves over the awful fate of France, still, her Colonies are beginning to start up well.

Love to you all.

KENSINGTON, LONDON
October 7, 1940

MY DEAR M.:

Last night I slept the whole night in my bed, which was a most delightful experience after weeks and weeks of a mattress in the lounge. The weather was so bad that the Germans did not come over after 8 P.M. They have battered down some houses in London, but they will never batter down our spirit; the people of all classes are simply splendid, utterly courageous, self-controlled and altogether brave. As for the day raids, which go on some days almost continuously, no one worries, except when the guns thunder badly, then one goes to ground. I got nicely caught in Belgrave Square last week; an air raid started about 1 P.M., it lasted 5 hours. I started off after 2 for the Depot, and had got as far as the beginning of Belgrave Square when the guns began to thunder like the devil, running was out of the question, weighted down by a heavy winter coat, huge parcels for the Depot, gas mask, bag, etc. One is very frightened of shrapnel, however I arrived safe, but somewhat flustered. When we were all wanting to leave, about 6:30, raid still on, but we decided to start, anything better than spending the night in an icy cold house and no food.

[315]

The telephone is not much good now as one is asked not to telephone when there is a raid on. As there nearly always is one, no one bothers; one only sees the folk one works with.

The Depot (French Red Cross) where I work is very interesting; one meets such a lot of types and hears so many interesting adventures. Three Frenchmen turned up today to be clothed who had come all the way from Cristobal on the Panama Canal to join de Gaulle's army.

The busses mostly run in a raid; 30 which does for me is very brave and never stops, 14 and 96 are a bit uncertain; they always go a tremendous pace, which delights my heart and of course there is very, very little traffic. I went from South Kensington Station to Piccadilly in about 5 minutes, good going. Saturday afternoon, my half-holiday, I do a jaunt. I thought I would go to Hurlingham and get some fresh air, however Putney Station was shut temporarily, so I then took a bus to the Zoo, because I have never seen the Panda or the Terraces, a long drive as the busses had to go queer ways, some streets being barred. I arrived and to my great disappointment was not allowed to go anywhere near the Terraces as there was an unexploded bomb in the middle of them. I asked the Keeper what he proposed to do if the bomb went off, knocked down the iron railings and let loose the bears. He looked rather vexed with me and only grunted. However I saw the Panda, a very amusing looking animal.

Theatres are shut, one or two give matinees. The Arts

Theatre has started a Ballet, quite good, only a shilling; one takes a seat an hour before and puts a parcel on it. I spent the whole of last Saturday there, from 1 to 2, 2:30 to 3:30, and 4 to 5. They empty the house after each performance and air it. Some very good dancers, *mise en scène* good, and it was so lovely to get away and forget the beastly, foul blood-and-thunder life one leads and talks.

K. telephoned me the other day from Scotland imploring me to go to stay with them there, where my precious life would be safe. Very kind,—thank you. But if one thing would make me quite mad, it would be to find oneself shut up in the country with nothing to do but twiddle one's thumbs and listen to the wireless, and the awful cold of Scotland now.

The barrage of London is now tremendous and the noise deafening, but we are very grateful. People often arrive in their nighties or dressed in oddments, as if a time bomb falls on a nearby house you have to get out at once. Some have gone off fairly near here, they make the house rock and quiver, rather like an earthquake.

Send me a card if you get this as I am often very tired and so it is an effort to write a long letter, but I thought you would be interested and as long as you get it, I will send you a line now and then.

One knows we are going to win, but I hope it won't take many years. Rather a beastly tragedy for the young to live through.

Much love to all, and happiness.

[317]

October, 1940

MY DEAR N.:

I have been wondering how you are? What you are doing? So do let me know how life goes with you.

M. wrote that he got down a Dornier yesterday, and he got a Messerschmitt a week ago. He has been shot down three times, once over Belgium some months ago. He had to use his parachute. When he landed he found it was full of bullet holes. The next time his engine was a blazing mass twenty yards away from the plane, he was unscratched, which was amazing, since he came through the side of the plane instead of the regulation way out through the top!

We all sleep in the kitchen in rows! B. and A. generally sleep upstairs if it isn't too noisy; however, a chimney stack got deposited in A.'s bed the other day so maybe he will stay down for a bit!

The church four doors down the street was smashed up, very noisy it was too.

A week or so ago we were having dinner in Chelsea where we had taken a flat, A. and B. were entertaining a relation—who had just been saying, "No damage at all, I expected worse" (maddening remark to Londoners!), when, with a great deal of noise, five fat bombs deposited themselves in the street on three sides of the block!

Two blew up just a few yards away but the blast went up so we were all O.K.

After dinner we went up to our flat only to be told

[318]

that two time bombs were sitting outside waiting to pop. (A Time Bomb is something which goes off sometime— not when it arrives.) Well, we left the flat and drove to No. 10 in a battle which would have done Mr. Goldwyn credit. Everything puffed, wuffled, wheezed, crumped and crashed—bombs whistled and screamed and "onions" and "lightning" lit up everything. (As someone said, the only people who enjoy this war are the gunners and they undoubtedly are having a wonderful time!) However, we got to No. 10 with only two large dents in the tin roof of the car.

London isn't too bad if you can sleep through the noise. This is a little difficult when we seem to have a few "Big Berthas" popping from the area basement, apart from all the other things that pop almost as close. It is really very odd how one gets used to things. Though it must be simply lovely to put on all the lights and open all the windows and see advertisement signs sparkle all down the street.

Won't it be fun after the war; you must come over and help us celebrate even if we are by then living in tents! It is odd about a war, the things that don't really matter, don't matter one bit! We do think we are your front line and if we don't stop Hitler you will have to do so later—it's O.K. though—we've got him taped!

DEAR C.:

As you see we are back again, the bombs having been removed from near the house, the one outside the office also has been dealt with. So now we are ready to settle down for the winter. We have been back for two weeks now, and are really quite anti-aircraft-trained to sleep by now.

Our garage has been shored up with timber and sand, and we have also done the maids' sitting room. One opens into the other. So we can all sleep in shelter. Indeed we somewhat scandalize our neighbours by even undressing. They all wish to be dressed if bombed. We take warm things, torches, gasmasks, and I even take a box of jewellery down with me each night, with the idea that if the rest of the house collapsed we could sell the jewellery to buy vests, as you might say.

The day raids are rarely alarming in this part or central London. And very often it is perfectly harmless though noisy at night. The sirens go off about 7.15 P.M. Now and then you hear the beastly buzzing diver, and then the guns go off. All sorts of noises near and far. Some nights this lasts an hour or so, then peace, then more pops. Others, like last night, bombs fall in the district. They always appear to go over the house before exploding, but the nearest to us so far has been at the junction of F—— and F—— Lane.

At about 10 P.M. we go down to bed. And that is

really more peaceful because there is nothing more one can do, so it is no good worrying.

D. [aged 16] is at home at present until Westminster moves—I believe to Herefordshire. His method is to pretend there is nothing going on at all. He refuses to go and see bomb craters or ruined houses, never raises his eyes to see exhaust trails in the sky and merely becomes more highbrow every minute. Last night he and G. read *Henry VIII* aloud, while I made evacuee clothes and the house rattled with gunfire, and the lights flickered when a bomb fell anywhere near!

October 16. This has been delayed by jobs. There is much to do what with the homeless people, evacuated children to dress and the like, and so many of the usual voluntary workers have left London that those in it are never idle. D. left for Herefordshire today. A. writes very happily from Oxford—very pleased with herself for standing up to a defeatist young man in a shop and making him admit he was wrong! T. [aged 12] is also full of bounce. He had done a day's potato lifting at Oundle and had been commended as one of the best farm workers they had ever had.

At present the night raids begin about 7.15, and though we are not among those who go into a shelter at once, we do stop indoors after that, for fear of shrapnel. I dare say we shall give that up with more familiarity.

Meanwhile I have picked up some classy bits round the house and what we don't return to make into more shells, is to be posted to your family in the hopes that it may amuse them! Here conversation is depressingly, or gloatingly, BOMB-TALK as you might say. M. has even found a badge which he wears on the inside of his coat lapel saying "I am not interested in Your Bomb."

You would be surprised at how ordinary London looks. Here and there is a heap of rubble and perhaps several houses with no glass, but usually it is just as usual. Where G—th works the story is different, I believe, but one never feels sure until you've been there, as stories magnify so. The word "gutted" sounds so well that it is used with great frequency but often with no grounds!

If it is fine on Saturday G. and I are driving down to Kent for the day. Officially to inspect properties, really to see our defences and with fervent hopes of seeing an Air Battle. We hear it is breathlessly exciting and wonderful what a handful of Spitfires can do.

The large craters on the Heath from which sandbags were made, are now being filled with house rubble—to the disgust of an old man working there who told G. it "wasn't right filling it up with people's 'omes, it ought to be with swept up leaves, it ought." To the less agriculturally minded of us, it is a tidy plan, and it's nice to see order returning anywhere. Not but what it wouldn't surprise you how quickly every hole is filled. It has its compensations, this semi-cave life. You feel so very much a Londoner and it feels very well worth being.

Hooray, the rain is setting in hard and it's 5.30 P.M. The last 2 nights the Harvest moon has been embarrassingly bright. Lots of love.

From a ten-year-old girl.

HOUNSLOW, MIDDLESEX
November 8, 1940

DEAR AUNTIE E.:

Thank you very much for your very nice letter and present which I was very pleased to receive. Grandma changed it for me at the bank and she got 4/6 for it with which I bought a pencil case and the rest I am going to save. I was very disappointed I was unable to come, as I was looking forward to ice skating and roller skating (I can roller skate). I am longing to see you again.

I am getting quite used to the air raids now but sometimes the bombs scare me when they are near. Mummy and I sleep at Grandma's now the air raids have started, Mummy sleeps in the drawing room where Grandma and Grandad sleeps, I sleep in the kitchen under the dresser. Grandma has an air raid shelter but we never go down it because it is damp. Auntie C. has a shelter and so has Mrs. B. but they are full of water now, so they cannot go in them. I must tell you that there is a lady who lives opposite us who used to go to school with Auntie T. when she was a little girl.

I had better end my letter now because the Jerry's have just given us a visit and they are still overhead.

Grandma, Grandad, Mummy and Daddy send their love. Give my love to Auntie T. and Auntie G. With much love to you all.

[323]

XXXXXXXX. Send Pog my love.

The fireworks are still going on outside and now I have to go to my little bed under the dresser.

If it wasn't for old Nasty I should be in a comfortable bed.

From an Air Raid Warden.

CAMPDEN HILL, LONDON W.
November 11, 1940

MY DEAREST R.:

I write so rarely to you that when I do it must be a long letter and I dare say you will want to hear something of how we are faring in this beleaguered London. (Sirens just going off, before 6 P.M. tonight, the earliest so far, I suppose the raid will continue now until 7 or 8 A.M.!) It is a hit or a miss—in a very physical sense! Some nights it is what we call "rough" and may be pretty continuous in or around our district, and on other, more blessed nights, we hear little more than occasional gunfire. When we are "for it," so to speak, there must be people in other parts boasting about their quiet time, and so it goes on. By day people pay little or no attention, in fact one cannot always remember whether it was "Mona" [the warning] or "Clara" [the all-clear] who last raised her voice. We have had our bad times here.

I am now living here where I have taken a most enchanting house and have gone so far as to furnish it, which a lot of people think mad, but, in a curious way,

[324]

one feels more human in this insane hurly-burly with one's own things, and if they are bombed—well they are bombed. The great thing is to live as normal a life as possible and in spite of living on a permanent volcano I wouldn't leave London for anything.

It is all very different to what I imagined it would be and at times more horrifying. It *was* one night about 1.30, when my house shook so that I thought it must come down. On going to the scene of the explosion it was difficult for the mind to grasp that where was now dust, rubble, broken glass, complete destruction, there, 4 minutes before, had been eight houses in tidy gardens. The night was exquisite and it made all the bombing around and the crashing barrage seem even more hideous. So strange that the small sapling trees still ringed the scene of devastation and flower beds showed unbroken shoots as if nature *alone* refused to be destroyed.

The most unpleasant smell in the world is of a bombed house. Apart from the invariable escape of coal gas, there is an acrid choking cloud of fine powdered brick which hangs about in the air for a long time and in fact never wholly leaves the wrecked building. One of the many unattractive jobs of a night like that is going into the half-tumbled-down houses and calling out to find if there are casualties of a minor nature from shock or broken glass, and you feel so helpless knowing that there are people under the vast expanse of débris. "That is my house," said someone, pointing to the mass of broken wreckage, "my maids are underneath." And the next morning when I went back to see it by the light of day, a macabre note was struck by a postman solemnly looking at names and numbers of houses on his package of letters and putting them back in his bag as the bodies of the dead were being carried away from the spaces in the row.

Our next incident was a few days later. Then the houses next to the Canteen where I was having supper were bombed to the ground. It is a strange feeling to be sitting in a basement kitchen eating tinned peaches and to hear the accelerating whistle of the bomb which you know this time is meant for you. Getting under the table or lying down flat is the recognized way to meet it, but we just sat—very very still. It seemed an eternity of carved silence before the explosion and blast blew in the window and with it clouds of choking brick-dust, coating everything and everyone with layers of white powder. There was work to do then, of course, so with the relief came a kind of tirelessness, almost I might call it elation. The tragedy beside us became so utterly impersonal, and it was a tragedy—five people killed and two out alive, but one—a warden—so badly injured that she died eight days later. She was 14 hours under the wreckage. Cruel that she lived at all. We all of us got a kind of delayed shock the next day. It took various forms. One of the wardens could not put on the wireless during the evening raids for a week for fear she missed the noise of her bomb! For about three nights I had to sit with the drawingroom door wide open. Neither of which could possibly do the faintest good but if that self-indulgence can get you past the next few night raids, they become a matter of course again—I suppose until the next time it happens!

It is sad to see so much wanton destruction in beloved London, but if our heads are bloody, they are still unbowed!

The two final letters are from a girl who volunteered as a Shelter Nurse in one of the poorest and most crowded districts of London. (The second letter was written on the back of several Government medical leaflets.)

CHELSEA, LONDON
November 21, 1940

MY DEAR J.:

One night, I reached Paddington at 7 o'clock, just as the sirens were wailing for the night raid. I hurried from under the glass roof into the hot breath of the underground and there they were, the poor people, stretched out all along the platforms, touching each other, sitting up eating their supper, some already asleep. The narrow path between the people and the line was crowded with uniforms, weaving in and out with the sideways motion one uses to avoid banging anyone with the tin hat on one's shoulder. The air was hot and highly-seasoned and thin. I thought I had never seen such a perfect scene for an Inferno, and an old Irish Colonel I had picked up in the train from Maidenhead stood beside me looking just like Mephistopheles, telling me he was descended from the Stuarts and inviting me to tea at his club. (His club has since been destroyed.)

Knightsbridge was closed, so I got out at South Kensington and was told the lifts weren't working, so threaded my way among the bodies to the stairs, and climbed round and round great iron spiral stairs covered with tramps; the air, as it got better, seeming to bring out the smell. At last I came out, trembling with the haste of my ascent, into an unmitigated blackout. I didn't know where I was for some time and stood in some street calling "Taxi," in a voice that sounded feeble among the gunfire. A man's voice close by said there were no taxis, and asked which way I was going, and said he was going that way too. "May I accompany you?" he said, and then, "Do you mind if I take your arm, or we will lose each other." So we walked briskly along, arm in arm, unable to see even a glimmer of each other's face. He asked me if I were in the Fire Service, and I said, "No, I'm a V.A.D. What are you?" "A soldier," he said, rather apologetically. He was going home on leave to see his mother in Battersea. No one could have been more courteous.

I'm in my fifth room since the Blitz began, having been flooded out of one, bombed out of another, left my two sisters in a third, abandoned by a terrified landlady in a fourth, and have landed in the eternal O——Street, a room that used to be the drawing room, with two long windows, well shuttered, gas fire, running hot and cold, two beds and a heavenly sofa. I love it.

You remember R—— Street in Chelsea; how slummy it was and the dreadful language that went on there, women cursing at their daughters, and such violence that C. said the Police only dared to walk down it in pairs a few years ago. I went through it the other day; it was quite empty and not a house remains habitable. Another day, to my surprise, it seemed full of life again. Soldiers cleaning up the mess were standing around bonfires, and the whole street echoed with jazz. It was coming from a house with the front off, like a doll's house, and on the first floor with a jagged edge, a soldier was playing madly on a piano. A strange sight.

In front of C—— Walk, a crowd was leaning over the embankment parapet, looking down on the little beach and there were the flock of swans, dark with oil, some dead, some feebly trying to clean themselves, all dying. A man was taking a few away in special baskets that close over their bodies with two handles that come together, leaving their heads out. It upset me more than anything else. They were so beautiful, and one had seen them so often early in the morning. They were being taken away gradually, I'm afraid too late. But what other country would care for its swans at such a time?

Another blow at the lovely things of life; they say the Germans are ploughing up the vineyards in France to plant potatoes.

[329]

PUBLIC SHELTER,
SHOREDITCH, E. 8.
January 19, 1941
11 P.M.

MY DEAR J.:

Perhaps I had better explain that I am now a shelter nurse, and have no other paper handy, besides which you might be interested to see the leaflets we hand out to the people.

3:30 p.m.

Having spent some time assisting a policeman's son with a very dirty face, and evidently corresponding rest, to get rid of something that disagreed with him, I now resume.

As I was saying, I have got a job which is so far most congenial. I hesitated a long time before taking it on. (a) Having a pre-conceived romantic notion, contracted in childhood during the last war, of nursing wounded soldiers. (b) A prejudice contracted in this war against the idea of public shelters; imagining the East End to be populated with tough guys who required a more robust character than mine to deal with them; imagining also an outburst of diseases from which I shrank.

So, I decided to go into a hospital. This decision put me in a very bad mood, as I realized it was pure cowardice. The crying need was for Shelter nurses. So I decided to try it.

Having received my orders, I shouldered tin hat and

gas mask, and set forth into darkest Shoreditch to take charge of the Medical Aid Post in a shelter under a big factory containing some 300 souls.

I arrived in the blackout, everyone in the bus having consulted loudly and most helpfully together as to where I should get off; made my way downstairs into a smell of humanity and disinfectant, and a shabby but cheerful crowd who responded eagerly with "Good evening, Nurse." I have become quite used to this undeserved title, and almost feel I am one by now. If the wielding of about 100 bedpans during the week in a hospital ward is any qualification, I am.

I have a room to myself in the shelter, with two beds, two tables laid out with my lovely new equipment, log, patient's books, stock book, etc., and entrancing cupboards of medicine to play with.

The people come in to me with touching faith, mostly, thank God, with nothing worse than sore fingers and colds. But we also have one suspected t.b. case, who will have to go to a private shelter or be evacuated if her tests are positive; two epileptics; and one pregnant woman, the source of much hope and prayer on my part. Have also had to deal with a small outbreak of bugs, and one of head lice. Both appear to be under control.

I have got to know the people and their babies pretty well—at first I thought I never would—there are about 50 children. Have so far had no trouble, and in spite of warnings, have had no thefts or impositions. They are amazingly cheerful, patient and good. Quite a lot have lost their homes, and alternate between shelter and work. Of course they are not very clean. There is nowhere for them to wash, they have chemical closets [toilets], drinking water, and a canteen for hot tea and buns, etc. They are still sleeping on the floor, but bunks have been installed in most shelters, and should be here soon.

A doctor comes round every night, and usually a trained nurse with him. Also the district M.O. looks in quite often, a charming man, who seems to be in a continual state of amusement which he hides under a stern manner; about 35. Excellent man for the job. A bright spot.

I work every other night, alternating with a nice young trained nurse, who keeps things ship-shape. It would be awful to have a sloppy partner.

This gives me a grand amount of spare time—It suits me to make one night's effort, and then have two days to recupe—I leave home at 5 P.M. and get back about 9 A.M. Usually I can sleep from 12:30-5:30. Not tonight on account of the policeman's son, who is sick every now and then, poor boy, and thrashing about a good deal. But he has no temp. and seems to be sleeping it off pretty well, so I'm not calling the doctor, although I can at any time. I called one the other morning at 5 for a child with a heavy cold and fever, and he came like a lamb without a word.

There is a police station above, which is comforting, and the police come in quite a lot. Many of them have such names as Epstein, Levy, Isaacs and Abraham. The

night of the big city fire two came in with inflamed eyes
from fire fighting—this was the first I knew of the fire. I
can't even hear the guns down here. When I went out
in the morning the sky was still glaring red through the
blackout, and great sparks were carried on the wind
across the streets. The traffic was hopelessly congested,
and I had to walk a good way, and finally went into the
Underground, which was solid. My hand was turned the
wrong way on the handle of my suitcase, and when I let
go to get a more comfortable grip, the suitcase simply
remained where it was. The train stood in the station
an interminable time. "Breathe in, everybody," called
out the conductor. "There's another one comin' aboard."
"Better get a shoe 'orn, mate," replied the conductor in
the carriage. Some people's faces were quite grey and
running with perspiration. The air was bad. A little sailor
was carried towards me, slightly on the bias, keeping up
a running commentary. "Na-then, 'oo's shovin' me? Stop
yer pushing. I'm surprised at you, you are a pushin'
young lidy!" To someone behind him; ending up in a
sort of reverie to himself, "Me feet ain't on the ground.
Pore little feller!"

I loved him dearly for that last comment. I wish I
could give you an idea of the way these people talk. I
don't suppose there is any more fertile nursery for music-
hall comedians than the East End. They are born like it.

It took me two hours to get home that morning. So
many of the lovely Wren churches, born of a fire, per-
ished in a fire.

I have a really attractive room in Chelsea, and in my selfish way am thoroughly enjoying life. Have had no personal bombing. My room is an ex-drawing-room in one of the O—— St. houses, with hot water, a good gas fire and ring, two beds and a sofa.

It is now 5 A.M. Soon I shall have a cup of tea, and must pack up, and dispose of this sick boy somehow. I suppose I'll have to ring up a doctor, as he can't stay here all day.

Sometimes one feels madly and idiotically happy. Our old contention still holds good:

> Now does our happiness,
> Frail golden centre
> Of a dark flower,
> Carry no less
> Than the living future,
> When petals today
> Of bloody nurture
> Shall fall away.